STUDIES IN AFRICAN AMERICAN HISTORY AND CULTURE

edited by

GRAHAM HODGES
COLGATE UNIVERSITY

A GARLAND SERIES

ACROSS THE BOUNDARIES OF RACE AND CLASS

AN EXPLORATION OF WORK AND FAMILY AMONG BLACK FEMALE DOMESTIC SERVANTS

BONNIE THORNTON DILL

GARLAND PUBLISHING, INC.
NEW YORK & LONDON / 1994

Library of Congress Cataloging-in-Publication Data

Dill, Bonnie Thornton.
  Across the boundaries of race and class : an exploration of work and
family among Black female domestic servants / Bonnie Thornton Dill.
    p.   cm. — (Studies in African American history and culture)
  Originally published as author's thesis: 1979.
  Includes bibliographical references and index.
  ISBN 0–8153–1542–2
  1. Women domestics—United States. 2. Afro-American women—
United States. 3. Work and family—United States.   I. Title.   II. Series
HD6072.2.U5D55   1994
331.4'8164046'08996073—dc20   93–6019
                                                                        CIP

Printed on acid-free, 250-year-life paper
Manufactured in the United States of America

To all of the private household workers

who have helped make possible my career

and that of other women.

CONTENTS

PREFACE

Almost fifteen years after this study was written, many social changes have occurred affecting domestic service; yet some things remain the same. Among the changes are the increased labor force participation rates of women and the resultant rise in the demand for private household help. The "shortage of good help" is not new but the growth of household cleaning businesses can be seen as a contemporary innovation. These businesses, usually owned and managed by White women, hire workers and contract with employers to clean homes. In addition to housecleaning businesses, there has been a growth in nanny placement and hiring firms which act as both employment agencies and employers. These innovations have occurred while the percentage of the female labor force employed in private household work has steadily declined.

Nevertheless, while some aspects of the occupation have changed, women of color, particularly Latina and West Indian immigrants remain over-represented,[1] working as independent workers and employees of some of these businesses. Household work is still stigmatized work and continues to be assigned to women whose race, ethnicity and class grant them few privileges in U.S. society.

Feminism has also brought about many changes in the last fifteen years. It has offered new ways of thinking about women's work; distinguishing paid work from unpaid work; analyzing housework as work; and challenging the traditional gender-based division of labor which makes women primarily responsible for household work and childcare. Despite these and other important first steps, feminism has failed to address the issues of unequal power and privilege among women inherent in any serious analysis of the structure and organization of private household work. With a few notable exceptions, theorizing about work and family which places low income domestic workers at the center has been done by feminists of color. These include the works of Elizabeth Clark-Lewis, Soraya Moore Coley, Shelee Colen, Evelyn

Nakano Glenn, Elaine Kaplan, Phyllis Palmer, Judith Rollins, and Mary Romero.[2] Their research has been conducted and published in the fifteen years since my study was undertaken. The scholars named above—sociologists and historians—have followed the pattern employed in this study, using the worker's stories and self-presentations as a primary means of gaining knowledge about the structure and nature of the work; its relationship to family; the role of race, ethnicity, culture, and immigration; and the dynamics of the employer-employee relationship, among other things. Their findings present a serious challenge for feminist theorizing, especially for that body of theory that seeks to make issues of difference and domination central to its mission.

Today, domestic work remains women's work and feminism has yet to confront the issues of exploitation and privilege that have resulted from the increased ability of professional women to hire working class women of color to do their housework. This anomaly and unaddressed challenge to feminist thought burst onto the public agenda in 1993 when newly-elected President Bill Clinton attempted to appoint the first woman Attorney General. It was revealed that she had hired an undocumented worker (referred to as an "illegal alien" by the press) and failed to pay the worker's social security taxes. This revelation, and the subsequent public furor which accompanied it, jettisoned Zoe Baird, the first nominee, and caused the second to withdraw. Then it became a benchmark against all other female and (in the interests of gender equality) male nominees were judged. Although the national dialogue about what came to be known as "Nannygate" sputtered out on the questions of hiring undocumented workers and the problems with current social security laws, the fundamental question of reorganizing housework, in a fair and equitable way for *all* women, was never addressed. Chicana sociologist Mary Romero refers to this absence of social responsibility for domestic work in the face of a growing need among working women for household help as "the housework dilemma."[3] She argues:

> Clearly, resolving the housework dilemma calls for more than the transformation of domestic service. As a society, we cannot continue to define reproductive labor as women's work. Cultural values and norms reinforcing equality must start at home with the simple act of picking up for ourselves. Beyond this, reproductive labor must be recognized as society's work,

a responsibility that requires collective responses rather than private and individual solutions. The goal must be to develop strategies to allocate the social burden of necessary reproductive labor in such a way that it does not fall disproportionally on the shoulders of any group.[4]

Across the Boundaries of Race and Class was one of the earliest attempts to examine the ways the structure and organization of housework as women's work influenced the work and family lives of domestic workers. As pointed out in the book, the women who were the subjects of this study exemplified a pattern of domestic work that was fading even as it was being studied: most worked for one family for twenty to thirty years. While only a few lived-in, the long term ties with their worker's families heightened the importance of the interpersonal dimension of the employer-employee relationship. Today, days work, a variety of employers, and what Romero refers to as "contract work," are the primary ways that workers participate in the occupation. These patterns occur as competition in the field shifts, the supply of workers diminishes, and the provision of services is being restructured by competitive, small-scale capitalistic enterprises. Contemporary analyses of domestic service must take these changes into account.

Thanks to the scholars mentioned above and others, we now have a richer database and more sophisticated theorizing about this subject. Today, the housework dilemma is a critical issue for a society that is undergoing major restructuring of women's work and family roles. In the fifteen years since this study was written, I have been engaged in thinking about and acting upon the subject of private household work not only as a scholar but as a working mother. I have raised three children from infancy to their teen years with the help of friends, family, my husband, my children, plus a number of housekeepers, babysitters, and nanny and housekeeping services. In some cases I provided written contracts, sick leave, vacation pay and social security benefits. I spent hours filling out social security forms and state and federal unemployment tax forms, then paid late fees when I didn't get the forms filed on time. I also attempted to help organize a chapter of the National Committee on Household Employees in my community. In addition, I have had workers ask for old clothes when I thought it would be demeaning to offer them. I have had workers create their own "uniforms" so people would know they were a "baby nurse." I have been told by some workers that they did not want me to pay social security taxes for them and that they preferred to be paid in cash. In short, I have personally lived on the horns of the housework dilemma and I remain frustrated and dissatisfied by the individualistic solutions available to most working women. It seems painfully obvious to me that the growth in working women has not resolved the problems of household workers and that professional women, especially feminists, have an important role to play in a social reorganization of domestic labor that will create more just and equitable working conditions for *all* women.

College Park, Maryland
July, 1993

NOTES

1. Mary Romero, *Maid in the U.S.A.*, New York: Routledge, 1992, p. 71.
2. See bibliography for complete citations.
3. Romero, *Maid in the U.S.A.*, Chapter 7.
4. Ibid., p. 171.

ACKNOWLEDGMENTS

I owe a deep intellectual debt to Richard Sennett, who, at critical points in the development of this study, challenged me to reexamine my assumptions, explore the complexities and contradictions of the data, and utilize my own perceptions and sensitivities in theorizing about the subjects' lives. His insights have considerably enhanced this study. Joyce Ladner's research, collegiality, and friendship have been a source of encouragement, support, and guidance throughout this study. Her careful, thorough, and probing comments have made an invaluable contribution to my thinking. I am deeply indebted to Pat Sexton, who has generously made herself available to me at various times throughout my graduate study. Her continuing interest in my work as well as the quality of her own scholarship has been an inspiration.

I would also like to express my deep appreciation to Richard A. Berk of the University of California, Santa Barbara, who provided funds for the taping and transcription of the interviews; to the Danforth Foundation and the National Fellowships Fund for fellowship assistance, which supported major portions of my graduate study. In addition I wish to express my gratitude to my colleagues in the Department of Sociology at Memphis State University for their forbearance and encouragement while I was completing this research. In particular, I would like to acknowledge Jerry Michel, Chair, who juggled a very tight budget and limited staff to provide some typing and photocopying assistance; and Lynn Weber Cannon, who has willingly read and commented upon many portions of this manuscript.

There are many other people whose assistance and interest in this study has made its completion possible. Most important among these are the women who willingly shared their life stories with me. Meeting and talking with them was both educational and inspirational, and I will be forever grateful to them for their cooperation. In addition, I would like to extend particular thanks to the directors of several senior citizens' day centers in New York City. Their readiness to introduce me to the women who visited their centers greatly facilitated my locating participants for the study. Their names and those of the women are not mentioned in order to protect the participants' identities.

Many friends and colleagues have assisted and encouraged me in my work. Several deserve particular mention. Among them, Sunni Green, whose friendship has been a consistent source of strength. She has shared the successes and failures of this project as if they were her own, and she has done everything possible, including assisting in locating subjects, to help me complete this study. Daphne Joslin, a fellow student, read and commented upon earlier portions of this research. As peers, working on similarly structured dissertations, we struggled together with questions of method and analysis, difficulties in locating subjects, problems of interviewing, and the challenge of completing a dissertation while caring for an infant. I would also like to thank Elizabeth Higginbotham and Carroll Seron for their friendship, collegiality, and belief in my abilities.

Finally, I want to thank my family. My parents, Hilda and Irwin Thornton, who with unbounded love and unquestioning faith in my abilities, have been a source of immeasurable strength and unending challenge. John R. Dill, my colleague, friend, husband, and lover, for his pride in my accomplishments, encouragement of my academic and intellectual pursuits, and willingness to give up rolls with dinner for the sake of my Ph.D. Last, but not least, I want to thank my one-year-old son, Allen Richard Kamau, who provided joyous relief from this research and the incentive to finish it quickly.

Memphis, Tennessee
October, 1979

Across the
Boundaries of
Race and Class

CHAPTER ONE

INTRODUCTION

The Research Problem

This study explores the relationship of work and family among Black women who were employed as private household workers for a major portion of their working lives. It focuses upon the perceptions and symbolic structures through which they present the strategies they used in managing work, family, and the interpersonal relationships involved in each. It also examines the ways they conceptualized and experienced social structural factors such as race, class, poverty and a low-status occupation. The study seeks to answer some of the following questions: What social meanings do the women construct for their behavior? How do they perceive the class and racial inequities between themselves and their employers? What do they reveal about their means of coping with these disparities? How were their perceptions of the work affected by socially constructed meanings of the occupation? What means did they create for personal satisfaction and reward? How did their work experiences affect their family relationships? What was its impact on their goals and strategies for childrearing?

A very special aspect of domestic work is that it brings together, in a closed and intimate sphere of human interaction, people whose paths would never cross, were they to conduct their lives within the socioeconomic boundaries to which they were ascribed. These intimate interactions across the barriers of income, ethnicity, religion and race occur within a sphere of life that is private and has little public exposure—the family. The family is such a privatized institution that many people never come to know intimately the dynamics of families other than those to which they belong through birth, adoption selection, or marriage.

Low-income Black women who worked in the homes of middle-and upper middle-class White families experienced and observed, on a daily basis, two very different life-styles: their employer's and their own. They became aware of the impact of material conditions on these different life-patterns. Their perceptions of disparities which could reflect back on the most intimate sphere of their own lives provide a unique opportunity to examine the impact of race and class on the family life of two different but interacting segments of the society. It also provides a basis for exploring, in very concrete terms, the nature of this interaction.

Childrearing goals and strategies is one example. The lives of the women in this study, whose work became a cultural and ideological bridge between different social classes and racial groups, provide important insights into the ways work impacted upon and was utilized in the childrearing process. These insights are particularly revealing because they focus on the concerns of a very special group of working mothers: those whose work involved mothering. The study explores their sense of themselves, their children and their work, and the ways in which each affected the other.

In order to understand the particular experiences of the individual women whose self-histories[1] constitute the data for this research, we must first place them within the changing context of the occupation, examining both its contradictions and limitations. We may then begin to understand the extent to which their personal experiences are a product of the nature of the occupation, their social class, their race and the particular idiosyncracies of their individual lives.

Occupation: Domestic Servant

Domestic service is women's work.[2] It is low-paid, has low social status and few guaranteed fringe benefits. The worker goes to work each day, usually to a private, one-family household. Most often, she works alone, separated from co-workers and subject to the personal goodwill and managerial skills of her employer with regard to duties, hours, and rewards.

Like the housewife who employs her, the domestic workers' low social status and pay is tied to the work itself, to her gender, and to the complex interaction of the two within the family. In other words, housework, both paid and unpaid, is structured around the particular place of women in the family. Ann Oakley, in her discussion of the trivialization and neglect of housework as a field of sociological inquiry, outlines the interaction of these issues as follows:

> . . . a *general* set of axioms is responsible for the place of women in the two areas of family and marriage and industry and work. The neglect of housework as a topic is also anchored in these axioms. They can be stated thus:
> 1. women belong in the family, while men belong "at work"
> 2. therefore, men work, while women do not work
> 3. therefore, housework is not a form of work
> . . . the third appears to be a deduction from the first two, but the syllogism is false. Its falsity hinges on the fictional nature of the dichotomy between "family" and "work" and on the meaning of the term "work." . . . Because work is not a component of the feminine stereotype, housework lacks any conceptualization in sociology *as work*.[3]

The dichotomy between work and family to which Oakley refers is a product of modern industrial society in which work takes place in the factory or office building and the home becomes increasingly privatized.[4] The private family came to be seen as a refuge from the world of work, its primary functions being socio-emotional and integrative and its activities considered to be immune from the bureaucratic rationality of the outside world.[5] It was within this context that the work women performed to maintain both their own households and a middle-class style of life was ignored in the sociological and economic conceptualizations of work. The domestic worker is, in some ways, an extension of the housewife. The housewife delegates some or all of her household and family maintenance tasks to the worker in exchange for wages.[6] While this makes the worker's relationship to that household distinctly different from that of her employer, the nature of the work and its position within the society at large affect both the housewife and the household worker in similar ways. Domestic service is women's work because housework is women's work. It is considered unskilled labor because it has traditionally been thought that any woman knows how to do housework.

Household work as an occupation has been shaped by these definitions of family and women's work. As a result, workers have been seriously limited in their employment opportunities, rights, and security. An article, written before World War II, expressed the then prevalent beliefs about the home and the position of servants within it:

> ... no fixed contract can be drawn up. For the home is a place where things cannot be regulated by rule and schedule. It is a place of adjustment, like the joint in a suspension bridge. . . . In short, the house is maintained for the advantage of the family.[7]

Even today, when the organization of household activities has changed considerably, a belief in the essential differences between home and workplace continues to inhibit the adoption of rational employer-employee practices in household service.

From Live-in to Live-out and Days Work

Many early writers and reformers on the subject of domestic service argued that the worker's status as a live-in member of the employer's household was one of the major factors retarding the modernization of the occupation.[8] These writers suggested that if workers lived out and came to work for a fixed number of hours as did factory workers, many of the abuses would be eliminated. As David Katzman has pointed out, the shift in emphasis from a live-in to a live-out system of employment and the "rise of the modern system of day work" occurred between 1870 and 1920.[9] The women who participated in this study migrated North and entered the occupation between 1920 and 1935. As a result, many had experienced both kinds of work arrangements. Their stories, therefore, provide some insight into an important issue in the literature on private household work: the impact of the shift from live-in to live-out work on the social position of the worker.

Erna Magnus, in a 1934 study of the social, economic, and legal status of domestic servants in Europe, Great Britain, and the United States, pointed out that living in the employer's household was the primary factor differentiating domestic work from other work and was a major contributing factor in the work's low social status. She pointed out that the worker was usually isolated from friends and family in an environment that was alien to their own upbringing, culture, and class origins. Because the job was centered around the performance of personal services, work-related duties and the idiosyncratic wishes of employers were indistinguishable. The result was an occupation in which the work was unstandardized, varying with the particular needs, demands, and personal traits of the employer. The individual worker thus experienced an irregular working day and received little respect for her own personal time since that could readily be supplanted by the demands of the employer.

Often the worker was a young, unmarried woman, a migrant from the rural areas or an immigrant. Living in the employer's household provided a place to stay and a way to save most of one's earnings. However, domestic work itself offered little opportunity for advancement. Once a worker had perfected her skills as a cook, housemaid, laundress or whatever, there were few places for her to go except to another house, with perhaps higher pay, doing essentially the same work.[10]

Magnus took great care to point out that wages varied widely with little regard for any systematic principles of economics. They appeared to vary with regard to the age and experience of the worker but also from house to house.[11] While the pay was competitive with women's wages in industry during this time—particularly in light of "in-kind" payments in the form of room and board—cash in hand, according to Magnus, was a more potent psychological attraction.

Finally, domestic work was frequently excluded from progressive and protective labor legislation and was generally ignored in the laws covering contracts of employment. Thus, work in industry was preferable with regard to such benefits as old age and health insurance, disability and unemployment benefits and workers' rights in the settlement of disputes. Magnus attributes this, among other things, to the lack of organization and collective bargaining among domestic workers.

There have been several attempts to unionize domestic servants in the United States and to make their labor "contract" more comparable to that of an industrial worker. Many of these efforts were short-lived and had little long-range impact on the occupation. Their failure was due primarily to the fragmentation of work sites which made organization and enforcement difficult and to the lack of legislative support for this category of workers. Dora Jones, Executive Secretary of the Domestic Worker's Union, explained the limitations on improvement in the occupation as part of a vicious circle in which the lack of both legislation and union organization thwarted improvement of the occupation.

> There is no doubt that should domestic work be placed under minimum wage and maximum hour legislation, this union would see vigorous growth. . . . The secret of it lay in the fact that once workers learn that they are protected by law, they are eager for organization that can prevent the violations they see going on. At the same time, with legislation passed, the union would be given a weapon to operate with. Workers would not only be given more time to attend meetings, but would more adequately afford to pay union dues.[12]

According to Katzman, the shift to live-out work was brought about primarily by the workers themselves, specifically by a shortage of servants and an increasing "dependence on Black and married women who preferred live-out or day work."[13] However, as he goes on to indicate, "this shift did not significantly affect the low status of household labor."[14] While this change did modify the working conditions somewhat, it did not affect some of the basic structures of domestic service and these, it became apparent, were more important in maintaining the low status of the work, than the particular organization of the worker's time.

The shift to live-out work did provide the worker with greater personal freedom, less isolation from friends and family, and more limited working hours. Nevertheless, today the worker still remains isolated in a private household and subject to the whims of the individual employer. Thus, the work is still unstandardized and arbitrary though its impact on an employee's personal life is somewhat less pervasive. Within this context, private household jobs are still dead-end jobs. Legal protection and benefits common to other industries are only beginning to be introduced, are slow to take effect, and almost impossible to enforce.

The data collected in this study suggest that women who lived out or did "days work" were less likely to become intimately involved in their employer's family life or link their own life to that of the employer's than those who lived in. On the other hand, those whose own families required considerable daily participation were less likely to take a live-in job. These findings tend to support the idea that live-out and "days work" did provide the worker greater emotional, psychological and physical freedom from the intrusions of the employer's family life. Since many of the women had done live-in work early in their careers as household workers, most had an opinion about it. In general, they preferred to live out or do "days work" and saw live-in as appropriate or perhaps helpful to a young woman who needed to save money when she started out. Many of their stories about this period of their lives stress their loneliness, isolation, and the difficulties in adjusting to being in an environment that was so very different from that which they had known. In their life stories, live-in work was, for the most part, an early phase in their career as a household worker, one which they had studiously avoided once they learned more about the opportunities and possibilities within the occupation.

The Personalized Employer/Employee Relationship

The locus of private household work within the family has retarded change in the occupation because the family is one of the most traditional social institutions. The privatized nature of family life in industrial societies, its apparent involvement in consumptive economic activities rather than productive ones, and its social construction as an arena for personal and affective relationships, hindered the growth of rational, bureaucratic, and universalistic principles of labor relations. Instead, the personalized employer-employee relationship remains a central feature of domestic service. Because the worker is isolated from other workers, the potential intensity of the relationship is increased; she is still susceptible to the idiosyncracies of an individual employer, and the worker's personality and human relations skills become as potentially important as her job skills. Her isolation within a hierarchical relationship results in a degree of employer-employee intimacy which has both positive and negative effects. Lenore Davidoff, in a discussion of domestic service, explains the relationship in this way:

> In any system of hierarchy expressed in rituals of deference, at a face-to-face level, there will be a continuing tension between identification with the superior (the giver of gifts and rewards) and social distance (protection of independence). How

far the subordinate identifies with the goals of the system and/or the personal superiors, and by so doing accepts his or her inferior place within it, partly depends on the rewards—both psychic and material—he receives but also partly on how easy it is for him to find compensatory definitions of self-worth.[15]

The data collected in this study indicate worker ambivalence towards their work and their employers. Their ambivalences center around the low status of the occupation, and their extreme vulnerability to the whims of an employer on the one hand, and the warm personal relationships which could develop through intimate participation in the employer's family life. It is within this context that their struggle for self-respect takes on importance because it is an outgrowth of the organization of the occupation itself and demonstrates the salience of personality factors. While employers searched for a person whom they thought would "fit" into their households, one whom they liked, were willing to trust, and felt could do the work, employees searched for "good" employers; those who were considerate, generous, and would treat them like human beings.

Katzman argues that the fact that the employer-employee relationship was between two women made it a distinctive feature of domestic service. The importance of that relationship in defining the job was apparent in the self-histories of the women who participated in this study, for it is their mistresses, more than their masters, to whom they referred most of their feelings of warmth, animosity, envy, disdain, and affection. It was she who confided in them, she with whom they shared personal intimacies, exchanged recipes and swapped stories about their children. It was her lifestyle they criticized most, her aloof manner which they detested and her insensitivity which inspired them to quit. Unlike other students of the occupation who have defined this relationship as paternalistic,[16] Katzman identifies "maternalism" as a more appropriate concept to describe the benevolent, patronizing, and "intuitive principles of management and personalization" which governed private household work.[17]

While it is true that many women saw their servants as children and "mothered" them in one way or another, this model does not fully encompass the relationship between the Black women who participated in this study and their mistresses, at least from the worker's perspective.

The stories of their early years in domestic service do not provide much information about the employer/employee relationship, primarily because this period was the one in which they were most likely to turn over their jobs rather frequently. Also, their memories of these early years were not as vivid. The picture of employer-employee relationships, therefore, is in the women's later years in the occupation, while they were raising their children or after their children were young adults. While the patronizing, beneficence of employers is presented, there is also a sense of the worker's ability to direct the situation, or to "mother" the employer who was often younger and more inexperienced in child care. Even if these accounts are largely self-aggrandizing on the part of the workers, there is reason to believe that race inhibited the ability of employers to see their workers as "daughters," and to mother them. Katzman himself goes on to suggest that in the South Black workers were likely to have considerable control over the work conditions, and in the North White mistresses perhaps adjusted more to their Black servants than the servants adjusted to them.[18] Other ways in which race impacted upon the occupation are discussed in greater detail in the following section of this chapter. However, it does appear to have modified the maternalistic aspect of the employer-employee relationships.

The emphasis on personal relationships both constrained workers and provided them with the tools to gain considerable control over the work. Katzman, for example, suggests that the shift from live-in to live-out work was a rare case in which workers had an impact on working conditions and that "quitting [was] the only way to improve conditions that was available to a servant."[19] The data collected in this study, however, strongly suggest that workers often used the personalized character of the employer-employee relationship to shape their working conditions to meet their own needs. The stories of resistance, which are discussed at length in Chapter Four, are examples. They suggest a process through which a collectivity of individual workers' demands have gradually, over time, and largely by default, resulted in a slight degree of standardization in the occupation.

A television commercial for a glass-cleaning product demonstrates one such instance of this standardization. The commercial begins by referring to a commonly accepted idiom that cleaning women "don't do windows." Implicit in this idiom is the notion of a stern, no-nonsense worker telling a frightened housewife, who is all too aware of the short supply of household workers, what working conditions she will accept.

The data collected in this study suggest that this image is not pure fantasy but has its basis in the strategies that workers learned to protect their health and welfare in a personalized work relationship where none of these protections were automatic and where market conditions worked to their advantage. While many of the women talked about washing windows early in their career, by the time they were "experienced" workers they no longer washed windows and neither do their contemporary counterparts.

The problem for workers has been to assert the values of the working world with regard to pay, hours, fringe benefits and working conditions within a structure largely defined by the quality of their relationship with their employer. This is further complicated by the fact that the employer-employee relationship is one of domination, one in which the interests of employer and employee are simultaneously interdependent and contradictory. Turn of the century employers preferred the live-in system of housework because it met their need to have someone on call day and night. As the availability of live-in workers decreased, they adapted reluctantly to live-out and "days work" because they had no other option. Nevertheless, live-out and "days work" met the worker's need to have a private life, uninterrupted by the intrusions of an employer. Mistresses accepted the live-out system because they needed the worker. However, the fundamental opposition of interests has continued into the present and its existence accounts for many of the employer-employee struggles which the women in this study described.

The Impact of Race

Racial and ethnic differences took on considerable importance in private household work primarily because the occupation was governed by both traditional and particulartistic criteria. For Black women in the United States, the occupation carried with it the legacy of slavery and they became, in essence, "a permanent service caste in nineteenth- and twentieth-century America."[20]

The heritage of slavery had an indelible effect on the growth and development of the occupation in the United States. In 1899, W. E. B. DuBois explained it thus:

In the United States, the problem is complicated by the fact
that for years domestic service was performed by slaves, and
afterward, up till today, largely by Black freedman—thus
adding a despised race to a despised calling. Even when White
servants increased in number they were composed of White
foreigners, with but a small proportion of native Americans.
Thus, by long experience, the United States has come to
associate domestic service with some inferiority in race and
training.[21]

Slightly more than a half-century later, C. Arnold Anderson and
Mary J. Bowman, in a study of the relationship of domestic service to
the South's status system concluded that the association of servitude
with people of African descent was the distinguishing feature of
domestic service in the United States. Through an analysis of the racial
and ethnic composition of the occupation by region and city, they
concluded:

> The American pattern . . . is distinctive in that the frequency
> of servants is correlated with the availability of Negroes in
> local populations, and there has been little change in the degree
> of this correlation.[22]

In the South, therefore, where the majority of the Black population has
resided, domestic service has been a Black-dominated occupation since
Emancipation, continuing to the present. This is due to a number of
factors; the lack of a sizeable immigrant pool is one, but more important
was the association of Blacks with service that was so pervasive as to
make household work anathema to any self-respecting, native born,
southern White woman.

The racial caste nature of domestic service in the southern United
States was indicated, Anderson and Bowman argued, in the dispersion
of servants along the income scale of White families. This contrasted
with other parts of the country where what they identify as a "class-
servant phenomenon" was more prevalent; Black servants were
concentrated among upper income White families and the size of the
immigrant labor pool was considerable. Theresa McBride points out that
the presence of servants was frequently used as an indicator of middle
class status in studies of the French and English middle classes.[23] In the
southern United States, it also functioned to establish Black and White

social positions. The servant role was an effective means of keeping Blacks in their place, emphasizing the superior status of whites, and maintaining the status quo. A similar situation has been pointed out by Margo Smith with reference to domestic workers in Peru, where the servant role becomes a means of reinforcing a traditional social status hierarchy.

> Domestic service is one factor acting to perpetuate and reinforce the traditionally rigid dichotomy characteristic of the social structure. . . . The servant role . . . has been and continues to be an effective means of . . . preserving the status quo by "keeping the Indians in their place" and reemphasizing the employer's superior status. . . .[24]

The impact of race on domestic service in the United States was not limited to the South, though it was clearly rooted there. The wide-scale participation of White immigrant women in other parts of the country suggested that class and ethnicity, in addition to race, were important variables. As early as the mid-1800s, under the impact of industrialization and the growth of capital, northern and midwestern cities grew and immigrants arrived to fill the jobs that were being generated therein. Many Irish, German, Chinese (most of whom were concentrated in the West) and Scandinavian women took jobs in service; jobs that catered to the urban bourgeoisie which developed along with industrialization. Thus, by the beginning of the twentieth century, domestic service was dominated by foreign-born White women in the North and Black freedwomen in the South, a pattern which was modified as southern Blacks migrated north. Nevertheless, as Anderson and Bowman indicate, it would be a mistake to see these groups as mere regional parallels. Immigrants fared better in the job market than Blacks and were preferred by most employers for the better paying, higher status positions in domestic service such as governesses and cooks. The relative success of immigrant women was largely a result of ethnic stereotyping. In addition, Anderson and Bowman demonstrate that racial caste factors in the occupation followed the migrants north.

> It is commonly asserted that the immigrant woman has been the northern substitute for the Negro servant. In 1930, when one can separate White servants by nativity, about twice as

large a percentage of foreign as of native women were domestics. Both groups were affected about equally by the varying proportions of Negroes in the population. . . . As against this 2:1 ratio between immigrants and natives, the ratio of Negro to White servants ranged upward from 10:1 to 50:1. The immigrant was not the northerner's Negro.[25]

Katzman points to two major differences distinguishing the experiences of Black domestics from that of their immigrant sisters during the period 1870-1920. First, Black women were more confined to domestic service with few other employment opportunities. Second, Black household workers were older and more likely to be married since urban Black women tended to work for most of their lives and their husbands' meager incomes required some kind of supplementation.[26] Thus, while domestic work, cross-culturally and for White women in the United States, was often used as a stepping stone to other working class occupations or a way-station prior to marriage, for Black American women it was neither;[27] a pattern which did not begin to change substantially until after World War II. Table 1 indicates that the percentage of working Black women in domestic service was increasing relative to the percentage of working immigrant women, which was decreasing.[28] It suggests that Black women were even more confined to the occupation than their immigrant sisters. The children of European immigrants, however, were much less likely to become household workers. Many Black women entered domestic service at that time, but their children remained in private household work.

The daughters of the women who participated in this study were among that generation of Black women who benefited from the relaxation of racial restrictions which began to occur after World War II. It is for that reason that their mothers' reflections upon their childrearing goals and upon social mobility are of particular interest.

Black women, as a group, did not fit the "ideal type" of a domestic worker: a young, unmarried, rural migrant or immigrant, utilizing the occupation as a stepping stone to upward mobility. Because Black women were more likely to have families, they were also more likely to choose a job or seek to structure a job in ways that would be most supportive of their family goals. Their attitudes towards their jobs and their mistresses were influenced to a large extent by their personal status. Katzman speculated:

TABLE 1

PERCENTAGE OF FEMALES OF EACH NATIVITY IN U.S. LABOR FORCE
WHO WERE SERVANTS, BY DECADES, 1900-1940

	1900	1910	1920	1930	1940
Native White	22.3	15.0	9.6	10.4	11.0
Foreign-born White	42.5	34.0	23.8	26.8	
Negro	41.9	39.5	44.4	54.9	54.4
Other	24.8	22.9	22.9	19.4	16.0
Total	30.5	24.0	17.9	19.8	17.2
(N, in thousands)	(1,439)	(1,761)	(1,386)	(1,906)	(1,931)
(Percent of all domestic servants)	(95.4)	(94.4)	(93.3)	(94.1)	(92.0)

Source: George J. Stigler, *Domestic Servants in the United States: 1900-1940*, Occasional Paper No. 24 (New York: National Bureau of Economic Research, 1946), p. 7.

> Married Black women, with their own homes and families, must have found it difficult to submit unquestioningly to the judgement of a housewife who was sometimes younger and less experienced than they themselves were.[29]

The data collected in this study confirm his belief. The women present themselves as not having submitted unquestioningly to an employer's demands. However, even if their actions were contrary to the stories they told, they clearly found that automatic submission to their employer's authority was difficult.

Like most domestic workers, the Black women who participated in this study were migrants. In their move from the South to the Northeast, they encountered many adjustments and found themselves working with people whose cultural heritage was quite different from their own. In New York and Philadelphia, one of the most striking differences for these very devout Christian women was to work for Jewish families. As a result, they learned a lot about Jewish culture, food, and customs that equipped them to work for other Jewish families.

David Chaplin has argued that domestic service was very important in the growth, maintenance and dispersion of the values and lifestyles of the bourgeois family.[30] McBride is quite cautious on this issue, suggesting that this process was not at all automatic.

> The identification of the servant with the middle class may be misleading. The extent to which servants were shaped by their association with the middle class or even consciously educated by their masters in middle class values needs to be examined.[31]

The women who participated in this study adopted and modified elements of their employers' lifestyles. For the most part, they imitated the things that they thought would help them or their children get ahead. As a group, they fit very well into the values of a middle-class society. They believed in the dignity of hard work and the possibilities of upward mobility. This permitted them to know and accept their station in life. However, they did not do this uncritically or without a keen awareness of the material and social inequities which made their lives so different from their employers. The data presented in this study provide some insight into the ways employees perceived and constructed the similarities and differences between their two families. It does not suggest a single answer.

NOTES

1. The term "self-history" is discussed and defined in Chapter Two.

2. Domestic service, as defined by the United States Department of Labor in 1939, referred to occupations of employees of private families, who are engaged in the rendering of services for members of the households or their guests. It included such job titles as butler, caretaker, chambermaid, chauffeur, child monitor, companion, cook, footman, furnaceman, gardener, maid, governess, handyman, housecleaner, houseman, infant's nurse, laundress, mother's helper, social secretary, housekeeper, tutor, valet, waitress, and yardman. (U.S. Department of Labor, U.S. Employment Service, *Job Descriptions for Domestic Service and Personal Service Occupations, 1939* (Washington, D.C.: U.S. Government Printing Office, 1941), pp. ix & 15.) While there have always been men in the occupation, the jobs most closely associated with cleaning, cooking and caring for children have been almost exclusively performed by women. Traditionally, most women who have worked in this field have been referred to as "domestics," "servants," "maids," and "housekeepers." More recently, domestic service workers have been referred to as "private household workers," a term which is considered to be less pejorative because it does not carry with it the notion of servitude and suggests that people who perform these jobs are "workers," on a par with other members of the labor force. The current definition of private household workers includes: housekeepers, practical nurses, domestic workers, day workers, house cleaners, grass cutters, handymen, window washers, chauffeurs, yard workers, cooks, companions, gardeners, laundresses, caretakers, charwomen, butlers, waiters, kitchen workers, and babysitters. (U.S. Department of Labor, Employment Standards Administration, *Private Household Workers: Data Pertinent to An Evaluation of the Feasibility of Extending Minimum Wage and Overtime Coverage Under the Fair Labor Standards Act*, submitted to Congress, 1974, p. 7). Within this study the terms "domestic service," and "private household work" are used interchangeably, the women are referred to as servants, household workers, maids and domestics, primarily for editorial reasons but also as a reflection of the terms the women used to describe themselves. The women who participated in this study worked primarily as housekeepers, cooks, laundresses, governesses, and babysitters. They

were not specialized workers but generally fulfilled several of these roles.

3.   Ann Oakley, *The Sociology of Housework* (New York: Pantheon Books, 1974), pp. 25-26.

4.   For a discussion of the impact of industrialization on family life with particular reference to the development of private family life see Phillipe Aries, *Centuries of Childhood* (New York: Vintage Books, 1962); Tamara Hareven, "Modernization and Family History: Perspectives on Social Change," *Signs*, 2 (August 1976):190-206; Barbara Laslett, "The Family as a Public and Private Institution: An Historical Perspective," *Journal of Marriage and the Family*, 35 (August 1973):480-494; Oakley, *Housework*, Chapter 3; Richard Sennett, *Families Against the City* (New York: Vintage Books, 1970), Chapter 4.

5.   See Talcott Parsons and Robert Bales, *The Family: Socialization and Interaction Process* (Glencoe, Illinois: Free Press, 1955); and Christopher Lasch, *Haven in a Heartless World* (New York: Basic Books, 1977), esp. Chapters 6 and 7.

6.   It is for this reason that the pronoun "her" will be used to refer to "employer" throughout this paper.

7.   Annie Winsor Allen, "Both Sides of the Servant Question," Social Services Series Bulletin No. 29 (American Unitarian Association [Ca., 1913]), p. 8.

8.   For a discussion of reforms in domestic service see: Jean Collier Brown, *Household Workers*, Occidental Monographs, No. 14 (Chicago: Science Research Associates, 1940); J. C. Brown, *Concerns of Household Workers* (New York: The Woman's Press, 1941); Erna Magnus, "The Social Economic and Legal Conditions of Domestic Servants: I & II," *International Labor Review*, 30 (August 1934):109-207 and 30 (September, 1934):335-364; I. M. Rubinow, "The Problem of Domestic Service," *The Journal of Political Economy*, 14 (October 1906):502-519; Lucy M. Salmon, *Domestic Service* (New York: The MacMillan Co., 1897).

9.   David M. Katzman, *Seven Days a Week* (New York: Oxford University Press, 1978), p. vii.

10.   Cooks were perhaps an exception because they could, and sometimes did, open their own businesses as caterers and restaurateurs.

11.   Magnus, p. 338.

12.   Quoted in Benson Ellis, *A Socio-economic Study of the Female Domestic Worker in Private Homes With Special Reference to New York City* (City of New York: Department of Investigation, 1939), p. 70.

13.   Katzman, p. 177.

14.   Ibid., p. 263.

15.   Lenore Davidoff, "Mastered for Life: Servant, Wife and Mother in Victorian and Edwardian England," *Journal of Social History*, 7 (Summer 1974):414.

16.   See Davidoff, "Mastered for Life," and I. M. Rubinow, "The Problem of Domestic Service," *The Journal of Political Economy*, 14 October, 1906):502-519.

17.   Katzman, p. 154.

18.   Ibid., pp. 195 and 221.

19.   Ibid., pp. 177 and 222.

20.   Katzman, p. 85.

21.   W. E. B. DuBois, *The Philadelphia Negro* (1899; reprint ed.; New York: Schocken Books, 1967), p. 136.

22.   C. Arnold Anderson and Mary J. Bowman, "The Vanishing Servant and the Contemporary Status System of the American South," *American Journal of Sociology*, 59 (November, 1953):216.

23.   Theresa McBride, *The Domestic Revolution* (New York: Holmes and Meier, 1976), esp. Chapter 1. For a discussion of the methodological advantages and disadvantages of this index of social status, see David Chaplin, "The Employment of Domestic Servants as a Class Indicator: A Methodological Discussion," paper presented at the Social Science History Association Meeting, Philadelphia, Penn., October 1976.

24.   Margo Smith, "Domestic Service as a Channel of Upward Mobility for the Lower-Class Woman: The Lima Case," in *Female and Male in Latin America*, ed. Ann Pescatello (Pittsburgh, Penn.: University of Pittsburgh Press, 1973), p. 192.

25.   Anderson and Bowman, p. 220.

26.   Katzman, pp. 219-220.

27.   For a discussion of domestic service as a "bridging" occupation for migrant and immigrant women, see David Chaplin, "Domestic Service and the Rationalization of the Household Economy," a paper presented at the American Sociological Association Meetings, 1969; Smith, esp. p. 193; and McBride.

28.   George J. Stigler, *Domestic Servants in the United States: 1900-1940*, Occasional Paper No. 24 (New York: National Bureau of Economic Research, 1946), pp. 6-7.

29.   Katzman, p. 220.

30.   Chaplin, op cit.

31.   McBride, p. 10.

CHAPTER TWO

METHODOLOGY

The basic methodological approach of this study was that of life history informed by the notions of the "sensitizing concept"[1] and the "constant comparative method of qualitative analysis."[2]

Life histories are particularly useful in studying Black female domestic workers whose stories and experiences have largely been ignored by social scientists.[3] According to Norman K. Denzin, the method "presents the experiences and definitions held by one person, group, or organization as that person, group or organization interprets those experiences."[4] Howard S. Becker provides several comparisons which give a fuller sense of the breadth and sensitivities of the method.

> The life history is not conventional social science "data" although it has some of the features of that kind of fact, being an attempt to gather material useful in the formulation of general sociological theory. Nor is it a conventional autobiography, although it shares with autobiography its narrative form, its first-person point of view and its frankly subjective stance. It is certainly not fiction, although the best life history documents have a sensitivity and pace, a dramatic urgency that any novelist would be glad to achieve. . . . As opposed to these more imaginative and humanistic forms, the life history is more down to earth, more devoted to our purposes than those of the author, less concerned with artistic values than with a faithful rendering of the subject's experience and interpretation of the world he lives in.[5]

It is perhaps this very diffuseness of form which has limited the use of the method to the exploratory phase of statistical research. While its value as an exploratory tool should not be underestimated, the life history has made a number of other contributions to sociological understanding. These were most forcefully demonstrated in the sociological work in the late 1920s, 1930s and early 1940s, conducted primarily at the University of Chicago.[6] To a large extent, these studies utilized the method as a way of focusing upon the study of "career." Clifford Shaw, for example, used this method to examine the growth and development of the delinquent career. Edwin H. Sutherland used it to explore the process whereby professional accountants become embezzlers. Utilizing life histories in this way, theoretical propositions emerged through the analytic induction model of inference, with each case providing a potential deviant case to test theoretically stated propositions.

A second use of life history, and the one which bears the most relevance to this research, is as a means of providing insight into the ways people experience institutional processes and social structure. The result, to use Becker's phraseology, provides a "check on our assumptions about these related processes, and also gives concrete meaning to the notion of process in sociological research." As such, the life history "describes those crucial interactive episodes in which new lines of individual and collective activity are forged, in which new aspects of the self are brought into being. It is thus giving a realistic basis to our imagery of the underlying process that the life history serves the purposes of checking assumptions, illuminating organization, and reorienting stagnant fields."[7]

I would go somewhat beyond this to argue that the life history provides a means of exploring the processes whereby people construct, experience and create meaning in both the interactional and structural aspects of their lives. It identifies and defines concepts appropriate to a sociological understanding of the subject's experience and can be an important first step in building theory that is grounded in imagery and meanings relevant to the subject.[8]

These histories, while structured around the particular concerns and interests of the researcher, were also left open enough to permit idiosyncratic differences to emerge in an individual's selection, organization and communication of her life story. To this end, they are seen as autobiographies in the sense in which James Olney defines them:

> An autobiography, if one places it in relation to the life from which it comes, is more than a history of the past, it is also, intentionally or not, a monument of the self as it is becoming, a metaphor of the self at the summary moment of the composition.[9]

Olney suggests that because the self is always in process, it is best defined through indirection,

> by observing an "experience" of the self, by seeking to create something that will evoke similar feeling or at least an understanding response in someone else. These somethings are *metaphors*. Autobiography is therefore a metaphor of the self.[10]

In this light, the stories which the women told can be seen as metaphors of their lives; their recollection of events, and their organization of them in a story which gives them meaning and structure at the moment of the telling. From an analytic point of view, therefore, we are less concerned with dates, places and names than we are with "a characteristic way of perceiving, of organizing, and of understanding. . . ."[11] The interpretation of their stories is also a metaphor arising from an attempt to connect their experiences with mine, with the experiences of other relevant social groups, and with sociological knowledge—itself a set of metaphors for human experience.

The term "self-history" which Daphne Joslin has used to define a "limited and brief autobiography understood as being significantly determined by the situation of interaction in which this narrative of one's life occurs"[12] may appropriately be applied to the data collected in this research.

Research Design

The data for this study were collected through interviews with twenty-six American-born Black women between the ages of 60 and 81, who worked as private household workers in New York and Philadelphia for most of their working lives, and who were raising children during their years of employment. In addition to the criteria of being American-born, over 60, and having raised children while working, participants were to have worked in domestic service for a minimum of ten years. While the racial and ethnic makeup of the occupation has always been much broader than the limitations placed upon the sample, Black women who were not American-born were excluded in order to eliminate differences of culture, language, and ethnicity that could confound the findings.

Older women were selected as subjects of this study for several reasons. First, as indicated in Chapter One, they migrated North and/or entered private household work when the occupation was in an important transitional phase. It was thought, therefore, that their life histories, set against the background of occupational change, would deepen the understanding of these changes by providing a personal perspective. Second, they entered the occupation when employment opportunities for Black women were almost entirely limited to some form of household service. Today, the number of private household workers is rapidly decreasing, and the children and grandchildren of women of this generation are employed in very different kinds of jobs. These shifts suggested that the stories of these women's lives might provide interesting insights into their perceptions of and strategies for social mobility. Third, there are the changes in the lives of the women themselves. It was anticipated that older women's lives could provide considerable insight into the interaction of work and family— particularly childrearing goals and strategies—by presenting adaptations to a variety of work situations and childcare needs not only between different lives but within the course of one life. Finally, one of the primary images of Black women in American society has been as a maid. Beginning with the mammy in D. W. Griffith's film *Birth of a Nation* and continuing through the character of Florence in the CBS Television weekly series, *The Jeffersons*, Black women have been depicted in this role.[13] Since the number of Black female household workers is decreasing rapidly, and over forty percent of all domestics were 45 years old in 1971,[14] there is reason to believe that the prototypic experience of Black women in domestic service which these women reflected is rapidly diminishing. This study, therefore, attempts to capture the stories that may soon fade away. The use of older women as subjects did raise some additional methodological problems, particularly because the interviews were almost entirely retrospective. The implications of this for the design and analysis of the data will be discussed in another section of this chapter.

The particular research problem which is explored in this study suggested the selection of a sample that would give heightened emphasis to the negotiation of work and family and at the same time illuminate the impact of the employer-employee relationship on this. It was thus determined that a sample of women who had worked in private household work for most of their working lives, particularly during the years when they were raising their children, would be most appropriate.

The Sample

The initial sample consisted of thirty-one women who were located by three methods. The first was through personal contacts; potential subjects were referred by colleagues, friends, or acquaintances who knew about the study. Eleven of the thirty-one were located in this manner. The largest group of subjects were located through senior citizen centers in New York City, specifically in the boroughs of Manhattan and Brooklyn. Sixteen of the interviewees were obtained in this way. Third, organizations of household workers in New York City were contacted, and this resulted in identifying three women. Finally, one was located through an employment agency that specialized in placing household workers.

The initially proposed method of sampling was a snowball sample, beginning with the women identified through personal contacts. However, when asked, most participants said they did not know anyone who might be willing to participate, or if they did, they insisted on contacting that person themselves. In follow-up conversations, I was usually told that the women were either too busy, unavailable or uninterested. The referrals from one household worker to others came through the women who were involved in household workers' organizations, as would be expected.

There are several possible explanations for the difficultly encountered in getting a snowball sample. Jeanne L. Noble suggested that "domestics do not readily identify themselves as domestics."[15] She argued that the low status of the work combined with the fact that some women may not always pay income taxes or may be receiving government benefits that would be jeopardized if their employment became known, could create problems in obtaining a sample. She also suggested that women who were working in these jobs had very little free time and were reluctant to use it for an interview. Although I interviewed many women who were retired and would perhaps have had more free time, they did not give any indication of having maintained contact with friends who did domestic work. And, while people may have been willing to participate as interviewees themselves, they may have been reluctant to identify a friend as a household worker, if that person was not in a position to identify herself. Finally, the personal contact and trust established during the interview did not seem to mitigate against these obstacles when it came to having the women refer a friend to participate. Only one of the women in the original sample of thirty-one who was not a member of a household workers' organization was referred by another subject.

Potential subjects were pre-screened for inclusion in the sample through the use of a brief questionnaire that was administered in person or by telephone before an interview was arranged. The pre-screening tool was introduced after it was discovered during the course of early interviews that the women had not met all of the sample criteria. An interesting observation which emerged from this pre-screening process is that many of the women who were eliminated at this stage were excluded because they did not have children. Although exact data are not available, this observation suggested that there might be some connection between a long career in domestic service and fertility, particularly as it relates to age at marriage, the restrictions of the job, and its potential for satisfying a worker's nurturing desires.

The actual data analysis is based on twenty-six (26) of the thirty-one (31) interviews. Four interview subjects were eliminated because it was later discovered that they did not meet some specific criteria of the sample (one woman was West Indian and three did not have children). A fifth interviewee was eliminated because the subject had exceptional difficulty responding to the questions. She was unable to specify many of the events she recalled and appeared to confuse people, time periods, occurrences, and locations more so than could be explained by the mere passage of time. Late in the interview she revealed that she had had a stroke which effected her speech and memory. I judged that symptoms of the stroke were reflected in the interview and that the data was therefore not reliable enough to be included in the study.

The Participants

As previously indicated, the women ranged in age from 61 to 80 years of age.[16] Most (twenty-one) were born in the South and migrated to the North between 1922 and 1955, with the peak migration being between World Wars I and II. On the average they had completed about eight years of schooling, with three having graduated from high schools or normal schools.

Most of the women came from relatively large families, the mean number of siblings reported being just under seven. Half of the women said that their mothers did some kind of domestic work, either taking in washing and ironing or working out in a White person's home. The other half described their mothers as housewives. Most of their fathers were either laborers or farmers. Their own families were much smaller. The mean number of children reported by 22 of the women was 2.43; in almost one-third of the cases there was only one child. While the women bore all of their children over a thirty-year period beginning in 1920, the peak childbearing years for the entire sample were 1930-1939. During the years in which they were most involved in working and raising their children, twelve of the women said they were married, twelve described themselves as separated or divorced, one as widowed, and one reported that she had never been married. Of the thirteen husbands for whom data are available, one worked as a chauffeur, one as a musician, two worked for the government (specific jobs unknown) and the rest were laborers.

These women worked in private household work for an average of thirty-seven years, the range being between approximately six years and sixty.[17] Two of them had worked for thirty-three years with one employer; among the rest, the average number of years with one family was 19.7. They characterized their duties as cleaning, childcare and cooking, in that order. At the time of the interview, eighteen women were either retired or working in some occupation other than domestic work and eight were still working as private household employees.

This brief demographic overview of the sample provides some historical specificity and an indication of how these women might have compared with other private household workers during this same period. While such comparative data are limited, other studies of household workers suggest that this was a rather exceptional group, particularly in terms of job tenure. Most studies of the occupation indicated that job turnover among domestic workers was exceedingly high and that women did not remain on any one job very long. Elizabeth Ross Haynes cited the following figures:

1890   average tenure of domestic servants in the United States: 1.5 years

1900   average tenure of Negro domestic servants in the 7th ward of Philadelphia: 5 years

1906-1908   modal tenure of Negro domestic servants in New York: 6 to 11 months[18]

Haynes also pointed out that the number of Black women in the occupation decreased with their increasing age. Thus, unlike the women in this study who remained in this occupation as they aged, the Black women Haynes wrote about either left the occupation as they grew older and as other areas of employment opened up, died younger, or as Haynes suggested, acknowledged the fact that it was not to their advantage to report their true age once they were over 45. In contrast to these findings, U.S. Department of Labor data for 1971 show that over forty percent of domestics were between the ages of 45 and 65 years.[19] These trends suggest that over the course of the last 50 years women have either remained in domestic work longer, lived longer and/or found no disadvantage in reporting their true age. While we cannot specify the reasons for this shift with any great degree of accuracy based on the data available, it does provide a clearer perspective on the women in this study as compared to the populations of current and former domestic workers.

The manner in which the women were chosen to participate in the study indicates that a degree of self-selection may have occurred. Since participants were volunteers, they were probably among those women who were most willing to acknowledge that they had done household work and to be comfortable discussing it with a stranger. By agreeing to an interview they indicated that they were perhaps among those least ashamed of having worked as domestic servants. While shame is generally associated with the occupation because of its low social status, an occurrence in one of the senior citizens' centers suggests it may be greatly exaggerated.

Upon arriving at the center, I was taken to a room where a number of women were sitting around a table chatting and sewing before lunch. The center director introduced me to the group, told the women a little bit about my research, and asked them to help me in whatever way they could. In response to my mention of domestic work the women sitting around the table began to talk to me and to one another comparing experiences. Openness and a general feeling of empathy and commiseration pervaded the discussion, and every woman at the table talked with me briefly about her work experiences, domestic and otherwise. There was very little indication that anyone felt too ashamed to acknowledge having done domestic work.

The Interview

Once participants were selected and screened, they were asked to agree to an interview that would take about two hours. Letters were sent to them in order to formalize the contact and provide more information about the study. The interviews were conducted at a location of the subject's choosing, either their home or the senior citizens' center. The women who were located through senior centers generally preferred to be interviewed there. They seemed reluctant to issue an invitation to their homes, a decision I attributed, in part, to a desire to get out of the house and also to the caution required of older people in low-income communities today. Nevertheless, they all gave their home addresses and phone numbers.

Most interviews were tape recorded and transcribed. The use of the tape recorder was discussed with each participant at the beginning of the interview. While they were encouraged to view the machine as an aide to me, they were also given the option of refusing to be taped. Only one woman, with a slight speech defect, asked that I not use the tape recorder. Data from her interview are based upon verbatim notes. Most of the subjects soon became comfortable with the tape recorder, appearing to forget it. However, at the end of the first interview, the woman, who had been referred to me by her employer's son, said: "You won't let _____ hear this tape will you?" I assured her, as I subsequently assured all of the other participants, that their comments were and would remain confidential. To that end, all interviews were given an identification number, for the purposes of concealing the participant's identity in the data handling process. In addition, names and identifying places have been changed in the data analysis.

The transcription of an interview is a tricky process. One loses the intonation, phrasing and speech patterns which are crucial components of a person's self presentation. Since I hired someone to transcribe these tapes, additional care was required. I therefore read all of the transcripts for accuracy, made revisions and corrections to more appropriately reflect the interview and checked them against the tapes at various points to insure that the subject's words were correctly stated.

While this discussion separates interviewing from data analysis, it should be stated at the outset that these two processes were closely related throughout the investigation. The data collection process began with some preliminary interviews in which general topic areas deemed important to the research problem were explored. From this, a set of more specific and elaborate questions were developed. However, additional interviews indicated that the processes of individual lives differed so widely that the questions had to be refined even further. The final interview instrument consisted of sets of questions grouped within general topic areas. Each topic area had a lead question supported by other subordinate questions which were used with much greater latitude and flexibility in the actual interview situation. The general strategy then was to ask all of the women the lead questions and to probe and explore their answers to each of these utilizing the subordinate questions as judged appropriate at that time.

This approach to the interview process was based on the objectives of the study, one of which was to identify the subjects' own definitions of their situation. Claire Selltiz, Marie Jahoda, Morton Deutsch and Stuart Cook state:

> The interview is the more appropriate technique (in comparison
> to the questionnaire) for revealing information about complex,
> emotionally laden subjects, or for probing the sentiments that
> may underlie an expressed opinion.[20]

In an effort to maximize insight into the subjects' intentions, feelings, attitudes, and behavior, each woman was allowed as much freedom as possible in organizing and presenting her life-history. Thus, an initial statement about the research goals, followed by the question: "Why don't we begin with your telling me a little about your work experience?" generated a wide variety of responses, ranging from a discussion on the theme of being a working mother to a resume of employment experiences. The result was that as each woman began to talk about her jobs, she created an individualized portrait of the meaning of work in her life, of the salient issues around which her view of work was organized, and of its meaning to her as a mother. Thus, comparability between interviews came to be viewed not in terms of different responses to a predetermined, carefully worded and consistently repeated set of questions, but more in terms of the totality of different lives and the patterns which emerged in the ways the women chose to present and reflect upon their experiences.

Aaron V. Cicourel provides the following perspective on this approach to interviewing:

> If the goal of the interview is to achieve some measure of "naturalness," then reliability cannot be achieved by the same procedures for all subjects but only for each subject taken separately. . . . Each interview constitutes a unique event in the sense that the identical conditions will not exist again for eliciting the properties called data. . . .[21]

The attempt, therefore, was to achieve reliability through an interview that was specifically responsive to the particular interaction occurring at a given time and place, to the definitions and meanings presented in each individual life and at the same time to impose some broad conceptual categories upon the process. For example, the focus on work has perhaps minimized some of the issues that these women would have identified as primary aspects of their lives around which other components were organized. Perhaps, had I asked people merely to tell me about something important in their lives, they would have begun with their belief in God. Their life history, therefore, would have revealed very different issues and placed the same experiences within a different interpretive framework. The epistemological questions arising from the notion that each interview is unique within the frame of scientific inquiry is an area where, in my mind, Cicourel's argument is weakest. Although he seeks to qualify this notion by arguing that a well-defined study should "transcend" some of the situational factors that can be anticipated in each case, he gives no concrete meaning to the notion of transcendence. My approach, therefore, was to keep these impositions at a minimum while maintaining some consistency between interviews with regard to broad questions asked and general topic areas discussed.

Cicourel's conception of interviews is based upon the premise that the interview is a process of social interaction and, as such, is governed by "rules of everyday life." Thus, he views problems of reliability and validity as fundamental to the process and irresolvable by mere manipulation on the part of the interviewer. He identifies five basic problems in the interview situation which he contends are endemic to all social interactive processes. These are trust; status discrepancies; varying perceptions and interpretations of questions; tension between polite discourse which maintains the interaction and the need to probe sensitive areas which may cause a subject to withdraw; and the fact that much that is meaningful to both parties remains unstated. While these problems, in his view, are never resolved, they are managed by all parties in the interaction for as long as the interaction lasts. Acceptance of Cicourel's notion of interviewing requires that the interviewer make explicit her assumptions and methods of managing these problems. At the same time, it requires self-conscious observation of the interviewee as to her methods of managing interaction.

With regard to trust, the women who participated in this study came to my attention either through someone they knew and trusted: the daughter of a friend; the chair of a household workers' group; the staff at the senior citizen's center; a man whom the worker had raised; or through personal contact as I visited the senior citizens' center, talking individually to women who were there. Thus, in some sense, I was not a stranger, a totally unfamiliar or unrecommended person, at the time of the interview. Throughout the interview, I tried to be forthright, telling the women exactly what my goals and reasons were for doing this study. Most of the women expressed interest in participating because they wanted to help me. This desire to help and support a young Black woman was expressed in many different ways. Some women were quite explicit about it and somewhat impatient with my explanation of the study's goals. They were primarily interested in helping me; and if this would help me get my degree, whatever it was, they were glad to do it. Others expressed their motives when they talked about the lack of opportunity they faced as young women. They expressed a sense of pride and satisfaction that young Black women now had opportunities that were closed to them. When one considers their strong commitment to education and upward mobility for their own children (see Chapter Five), the motivation to help me becomes even more understandable. No one was paid for their participation, nor was there any mention of any other kind of remuneration.

The problem of trust provides additional insight into the kind of self-selection factors which were operative in obtaining this sample. Among the women I talked with informally in senior citizens' centers, most were supportive and encouraging and answered my pre-screening questions without any appearance of suspicion. There were, I am sure, some women who were household workers but never identified themselves as such, and a few others withdrew after having initially agreed to participate. One woman implied that she had had a child out of wedlock and did not wish to be interviewed about her life. Another woman virtually disappeared from the center on the day I was scheduled to interview her, without any explanation. A third woman who would not give me her address but talked with me on the telephone several times never seemed able to find time for an interview. In addition, there were several women who were willing to sit and chat in the centers but were unwilling to arrange for a more "formal" interview. In general, the women who chose to participate in this study were more inclined to trust and want to help me from the outset; those who refused were more suspicious either of a "structured" interview or of my overall objectives and were unwilling to review their life with a stranger.

Whatever status disequilibrium existed in these interviews probably worked in the subjects' favor. They tended to look upon me as a daughter or niece, occasionally invoking their superior age, experience, and special status as informants. My education and affiliation with a major university in the area did not appear to outweigh my youth.

I attempted to handle the problem of varying interpretations of questions by continually refining them throughout the early phases of the data collection process and by asking women to expand and reflect upon statements during the interview. This, of course, did not eliminate the problem, but it helped control it and provided me with additional data to use in interpreting the subject's meaning.

By far the most difficult problem was managing the tension between "polite" conversation and the demands of the study. On several occasions I found myself listening to stories about family pets and hesitating to interrupt or change the subject for fear or being considered rude and insensitive. While this seemed to be a major weakness in my interviewing at the outset, I did improve and was able to shift the

balance more toward my own objectives than I had been able to do at
first.

In reviewing the transcripts and interview notes, I tried to look
carefully at the strategies various women used to test our relationship
or to structure the interview in a way that suited their needs. One
woman, for example, began by asking me a lot of questions about what
kinds of answers would be considered acceptable. She was particularly
concerned that she would not have to mention anyone's name. Another
respondent turned to me, after answering a question I had asked, and
said: "What do *you* think?" When I realized that she was testing me as
well as the acceptability of her answer, I replied that she had made an
interesting point, one I had never thought of before but one that did
make sense to me. That was an honest answer. On several other
occasions, women asked my opinion on matters I had raised with them.
My approach was to answer as directly as I could without implying a
negative or positive judgement of their response.

In addition to these problems, which Cicourel says are basic to
interviewing, there are several problems specific to this study which
further confound the reliability and validity of the data. The first of
these has to do with the fact that most of the data is retrospective.
Recognizing that age, temporal distance from an event, general
competency, and historical conditions operative at the time all affect
recall, this is a particularly important problem in assessing the quality
of data that were collected. In addition, unlike the oral historian who is
seeking verbal descriptions of events documented in the historical
records, the events which are the subject of these interviews were
observed by very few people and were unlikely to be recorded
anywhere, perhaps not even in the person's memory. In fact, the things
which we call events are really one woman's perception of occurrences
and they are presented because she considered them important or
noteworthy in her own history. Others who participated in the same
occurrences may not have considered them either important or
noteworthy enough in *their* life or in *their* interaction with the subject
to have remembered them at all. In addition, if they did remember them,
they might recall them quite differently.

While I have sought to rely on the internal consistency of the
individual story as a measure of its validity, I have also utilized some
techniques of oral history and a modification of Robert Merton and
Patricia L. Kendall's concept of retrospective introspection[22] to

encourage the interviewees in remembering past events. Basically, people were asked to interrelate past events, to talk about a job they had when their child was school age or to talk about who cared for a child before he/she started school, and to relate that to a job, employer and a particular set of experiences they had previously described. In addition, however, I have had to rely on my own judgement of the respondent's memory. This, however, was not an entirely arbitrary process since I did all of the interviewing myself, had some sense of each participant's motives for participating in the study, and directly observed their interaction with me. It became apparent that some people were better subjects for life history than others. The ability to recall and describe past events graphically and in detail, the willingness to elaborate on one's thoughts and to be self-critical and reflective about one's behavior yielded the richest interview data. Increasingly, I judged and weighed the data on these criteria. My objective in the interview was to create a climate of trust and frankness that could encourage the participant to use these abilities.

In addition, however, I have sought to read the data not so much as an account of a series of factual events but as a presentation of an individual life which was shared with the interviewer at a specific historical moment. The actual occurrences, therefore, are less important to the goals of the study than a women's perception of these events. To repeat a much-quoted statement of W. I. Thomas:

> There may be, and there is, doubt as to the objectivity and veracity of the record, but even the highly subjective record has value for behavior study. . . . If men define situations as real, they are real in their consequences.[23]

The events which people described in recollecting their experiences as domestic workers had consequences for their entire lives—at least as they saw it and were willing to share it at the time of the interview. Thus, their recollections of their lives were very much shaped by the circumstances, personal and historic, which were operative at the time of the interview.

The age and stage of life of the subject at the time of the interview must also be taken into account. The stories which they told about their lives reflected their present status. Those who had achieved a degree of comfort and satisfaction with themselves and their children were more likely to present a positive and hopeful story. Those who had been

severely disappointed or hurt were more likely to appear bitter and/or
defeated. In analyzing the data I have tried to make my interpretation
of a woman's state of mind explicit whenever necessary.

Changing historical circumstances of Black people in general and
household workers specifically have also had impact on the ways the
women saw their work. This was perhaps most apparent among the
women who were actively involved in organizations of household
workers. They identified changes in their own attitudes toward both the
work and their employers which they attributed to their participation in
these groups. In fact, they were more likely to discuss the work in terms
of exploitation and injustice and to see it as a social rather than a
personal issue. On the other hand, there were several women who
assured me they had "no bad stories" to tell, as if the general view of
the work today was that the only interesting stories about domestic work
were stories of mistreatment and exploitation.

Finally, I recognize that I asked the women to share something
about their life with me. The data I collected are what they were willing
to share. It reflects how they saw themselves as well as how they
wanted me to see them, and brings us, full circle, back to the basic
problems of social interaction. It is for this reason that I thought it
important, in Chapter Four for example, to discuss the stories of
resistance. They represent a prevalent pattern in the way the women
presented themselves to me in the course of the interview. It also
represents an important aspect of the ways they chose to see themselves
in relationship to their work.

Data Analysis

It should be clear at this point that data analysis was an integral
part of the process of data collection and relied heavily upon the ways
in which the texts of each interview were read. The approach to analysis
followed some of the basic principles of the constant comparative
method of qualitative analysis as outlined by Barney Glaser and Anselm
Strauss,[24] permitting major analytic concepts to emerge from the data
through the process of comparison across subjects and within categories.

While data collection was organized into broad categories, the
process of data analysis focused upon redefining or refining these
categories. The first step was to write case studies of carefully selected
and ostensibly different lives. These studies, when compared, generated

a series of "problematics"—questions framed as problems requiring resolution—which were used in reading, comparing and organizing the remainder of the data. With regard to work, the "problematic" related to women's strategies for maintaining and communicating self-respect within a stigmatized occupation. Within the area of childrearing, a major question was the way in which the women perceived, described and experienced the disparities between their children's lives and opportunities and those of the employers' children.

Utilizing these questions as initial approaches to coding the data, concepts began to emerge which explained the patterns and differences in a category. The notion that some workers had careers in domestic service while others did not, that some became surrogate mothers while others did not, that some told stories of resistance while others did not, are some examples.

A discussion of these patterns and of the ways in which the women in this study responded to the problems that defined their experience is presented in detail in the following three data chapters.

NOTES

1. Norman K. Denzin, *The Research Act* (Chicago: Aldine, 1970), pp. 14-15.

2. Barney Glaser and Anselm Strauss, *The Discovery of Grounded Theory* (Chicago: Aldine, 1967), Chapter 5.

3. There is a very limited body of literature directly focused upon Black women in domestic service in the United States. Many of these studies are confined to the southern experience. Among the most important studies containing data on Black women in northern cities are: Elizabeth Ross Haynes, "Negroes in Domestic Service in the United States," *Journal of Negro History*, 8 (October, 1923):384-442; Isabel Eaton, "Negro Domestic Service in Seventh Ward Philadelphia," in W. E. B. DuBois, *The Philadelphia Negro* (1899; reprint ed.; New York: Schocken Books, 1967); David Chaplin, "Domestic Service and the Negro," in Arthur Shostak and William Gamberg, eds., *Blue Collar World* (Englewood Cliffs, N.J.: Prentice-Hall, 1964).

Some discussion of the subject was also found in community studies, particularly those conducted before World War II. For example: St. Clair Drake and Horace Cayton, *Black Metropolis* (New York: Harper and Row, 1945); Mary White Ovington, *Half a Man* (New York: Longman's, Green, and Co., 1911; reprint ed., New York: Schocken Books, 1969). Labor studies provided a third source of data. Among these were: Lorenzo J. Greene and Carter G. Woodson, *The Negro Wage Earner* (Washington, D.C.: The Association for the Study of Negro Life and History, Inc., 1930); George Haynes, *The Negro at Work in New York City: A Study in Economic Progress* (New York: Longman's, Green, and Co., 1912).

4.   Denzin, p. 220.

5.   Howard S. Becker, *Sociological Work* (Chicago: Aldine, 1970), pp. 63-64.

6.   See W. I. Thomas and Florian Znaniecki, *The Polish Peasant* (Boston: The Gorham Press, 1918); Clifford Shaw, *The Jack Roller* (1930; reprint ed., Chicago: University of Chicago Press, 1966); Edwin H. Sutherland, *The Professional Thief* (Chicago: University of Chicago Press, 1937).

7.   Becker, p. 70.

8.   This discussion is drawn largely from a paper by Bonnie Thornton Dill and Daphne Joslin, "The Limits of Quantitative Methods: The Need for Life Histories," presented at the Society for the Study of Social Problems Annual Meetings, Chicago, September, 1977.

9.   James Olney, *Metaphors of Self* (Princeton, New Jersey: Princeton University Press, 1972), p. 35.

10.   Ibid., pp. 29-30.

11.   Ibid., p. 37.

12.   Daphne Joslin, "Working Class Daughters, Middle Class Wives: Social Identity and Self-Esteem Among Women Upwardly Mobile Through Marriage" (Ph.D. dissertation, New York University, 1979), Chapter 2.

13.   For a discussion of film images of Black women as servants see Donald Bogle, *Toms, Coons, Mulattoes, Mammies, and Bucks* (New York: Viking Press, 1973), Chapter 3.

14.   U.S. Department of Labor, Employment Standards Administration, *Private Household Workers*, submitted to Congress, 1974, p. 36.

15.   Jeanne L. Noble, "An Exploratory Study of Domestics' View of Their Working World," prepared for the Office of Manpower Policy, Evaluation and Research, U.S. Department of Labor, Manpower Administration, 1967 (mimeographed), p. 46.

16.   The women who participated in this study were interviewed between January and October, 1976.

17.   Although the minimum cut-off for the sample was originally ten years, it was discovered in the course of the interviews that a number of women could not accurately specify the years they had worked in domestic service, particularly if it was a long time ago and they had worked in other jobs since that time. This occurred only in cases of non-career women. See Chapter Four for a definition of non-career women.

18.   Elizabeth Ross Haynes, "Negroes in Domestic Service," p. 393.

19.   U.S. Department of Labor, Employment Security Administration, p. 36.

20.   Claire Selltiz, Marie Jahoda, Morton Deutsch and Stuart Cook, *Research Methods in Social Relations* (New York: Holt, Rinehart and Winston, 1959), p. 242.

21.   Aaron V. Cicourel, *Method and Measurement in Sociology* (New York: Free Press of Glencoe, 1964), pp. 80-81.

22.   Robert Merton and Patricia L. Kendall, "The Focused Interview," *American Journal of Sociology*, 51 (May, 1946):541-557.

23.   W. I. Thomas and Florian Znaniecki, *The Polish Peasant in Europe and America* (Boston: The Gorham Press, 1918).

24.   Glaser and Strauss, Chapters 2 and 5.

CHAPTER THREE

LIVES: THREE CASE STUDIES

Comparative analyses of this collection of individual life stories was the major procedure used in analyzing the present data. This procedure, however, begins with particular lives; with the stories individual women told about their struggles, crises, hopes and aspirations; with their answers to my questions. A thematic approach to the data, while illuminating some issues, does not do justice to the women as individuals. This presentation of three individual life stories has been undertaken in order to more fully convey the texture and flavor of the women's lives.

The women whose stories are recreated below were selected because their lives reveal the variety within the data in terms of the objective conditions of work and family life. While their stories are unique expressions of their individual experiences, they are particularly important because they reveal and illuminate themes which are recurrent throughout the data. To this extent, these women are prototypes of other participants of this study. Here, as with all of the data, the names used are fictitious, the women's comments have been edited for clarity and readability, and in some instances, phrases may have been omitted or thoughts rearranged in an effort to achieve maximum lucidity. These editorial changes have been made gingerly, while attempting to remain as true to the women's original words as possible.

The first life story is that of Lena Hudson. She worked for only two families over a period of forty-three years and was employed full-time in both homes but never lived in. She described herself as a general housekeeper on her first job and as a governess in the last one. She separated from her husband while her children were young and raised all four of them by herself while working. At the time of the interview, she was 80 years old and had retired.

Jewell Prieleau, whose story is second, had worked for over thirty years with one family as a live-in housekeeper and was still living and working in that household at the time of the interview. As a young woman, she had left the father of her child and migrated North, leaving the child in the South to be raised by relatives with the aid of the money she earned as a housekeeper. Although she had been separated from her daughter during most of the girl's childhood, she later became a central figure in raising her daughter's children.

Finally, there is Opallou Tucker. Mrs. Tucker described herself as a day worker. She did private household work for almost forty years but worked at different jobs each day of the week. For twenty-seven of those years she had worked as a laundress with one family, two or three days a week, and as a general housecleaner in other homes and apartments on the remaining days. She had also worked as a caterer's helper. She and her husband of forty-two years had raised four children and bought a home together. He had died only a few years before the interview. When interviewed, she was still working but had left private household work to work as a kitchen aide in a school.

Lena Hudson

> Well, I can't say it was a hard life because I was able to work and do the little things that I wanted to do. What I was able to do, I was able to accomplish, you know. It may seem little to some people, but it was a great thing for me to give my children enough education so they could make a livin' for themselves. And they appreciate it and they are good children and it makes a good life for me now. So I have no complaints. No complaints.

Lena Hudson made this statement near the end of an interview in which she had discussed raising four children by herself, caring for an invalid mother, being on and off public assistance, and experiencing major marital frustrations. By most objective standards, she did have a hard life. Yet at 80 years of age, she looked back on it without complaint, saying she could not call it hard.

One reads this statement in light of the problems she confronted during her life and wonders if Mrs. Hudson has not merely rationalized or repressed the pain and anguish of that period. Perhaps, in some ways, she has. The fact that her children became the kind of adults that she wanted them to become does permit her to look back on her life with a sense of pride and accomplishment. These present satisfactions have probably had a mellowing effect on the struggles of the past. But more importantly, Mrs. Hudson's view of life at 80 reflects an attitude which is pervasive throughout her life history. It is a sense of self-determination, a belief that one can set goals and achieve them even in the face of obstacles and crises over which one has little control. The statement above does not convey either fatalism or determinism. It is, instead, a celebration of her abilities: the ability to work, to do the things she wanted to do, and most important, to achieve the goals she had set for her children.

Lena Hudson described childrearing in terms of very specific goals and strategies. She expressed her early aspirations for her children as follows:

> I wanted them to be something. I didn't want 'em to be children that ran around in the street and got in bad company. You know, lots of times that changes the children. And so that was the standard: I just wanted 'em to be a good decent person. And by putting them in things that I thought would help mold them, I put them in it. And I think that's the principle of life with any mother if she wants to see her children . . . she must want to be something herself. And if she can't make the grade she wants to be, put your children . . . I think that's one of the reasons that I had good children because I tried to live that life before them. And I never had any trouble. They all four of 'em were born right in New York.

This statement conveys her major concern as a mother, how to expose her children to "good" things and protect them from "bad" influences when she had to be away from home at work and when the environment held many temptations. One of her strategies is expressed in the statement below:

> I haven't had any trouble with my children, thank God. They were all good children. And I enjoyed my work and I enjoy children. Being a member of Berean Church here—my children were small, they all were in Girl Scouts and sang in the choir—and that kept them busy. So all the time I worked, my children never had a key around their necks.

Having a "key around their necks" represents not only a lack of supervision and control over the children, but a lack of protection. It is one of the things she sought most to avoid. In her own words:

> They never was thrown out, like on the city—not like me working they had to roam the streets until I'd come home, you know.

Mrs. Hudson was quite aware of the dangers that the city held for young Black children, of its potential for turning good children into bad ones. So, part of the way in which she worked towards having good children was to utilize institutions and people who could provide babysitting and protective services and, at the same time, reinforce the values which she sought to instill in the children. Berean Church, which was about seven blocks from her home, was one of these. She says:

> They (the children) would come to the church after school and they were here during the time I'd get off, sometime around four o'clock. And I was home to make dinner. I must say this church has meant so much to me and my family. The activities they had here that kept my children. I think by putting them in church here, and they were around good things, that's why I haven't had any trouble with them.

The goals which she selected for her children—that they could become decent people and that they attain "enough education so that they could make a livin' for themselves"—appear quite modest. Yet they were not. Accomplishing them required as much of her time, commitment and creativity as a medical education would have required money. In the statement which opens this chapter, she says the following about educating her children: "It may seem little to some people, but it was a great thing for me. . . ."

On one level, her concern that the children be "good" and stay out of "trouble" was a desire that they become clean-living, law-abiding citizens. But on another level, this concern may be interpreted as reflecting a primary interest in their character development. As the focus of childrearing practices, it contrasts with middle-class parental goals which tend to be geared more towards career or occupational objectives external to the child's character. This difference suggests Mrs. Hudson's recognition, at some level, of the social realities which shaped her life and would affect her children in one way or another. One may surmise that it was not only an adaptation to limited means which made career goals seem out of reach, but a necessity that she give serious attention to developing individuals who had the strength of character needed to survive in a racist society.

At the same time, however, Mrs. Hudson worked hard to help her children attain an educational level that could make their survival less difficult than her own. Thus, while she did not describe any specific career objectives which she had held for her children, she did describe, with pride, their occupational accomplishments.

> He (the son) works for the subway, and the twin to him, she was a telephone operator until she got married, then she was home. My oldest is a medical secretary for a doctor, and the youngest daughter, she's a secretary.

One of the most striking things about Lena Hudson is that the goals which she set for her children and for herself reflect both active self-determination as well as a realistic assessment of the circumstances which bounded her life. Her language is active and generally unembittered. Her philosophy is largely one of taking what you have and making the best out of it. When asked, "What do you think were the goals that the Wallises (her employers) had for their children? What did they want for their children? What did they want them to become in life?" she replied:

> Well for *their* children, I imagine they wanted them to become like they were, educators or something that-like [*sic*]. But what they had in for *my* children, they saw in me that I wasn't able to make all of that mark but raised my children in the best method I could. Because I wouldn't have the means to put *my* children through like they could for *their* children. And they see I wasn't the worst person in the world, and they saw I meant *some* good to my family, you see, so I think that was the standard with them and my family.

Her answer to this question provided insight into the personal and social relationship between the two families and into the recognition of the points of connectedness and distance between them. The way in which she chose to answer the question reflects her feelings about working for the Wallis family and how that helped her accomplish the goals which she had set for her own family. Mrs. Hudson went on to say:

> They (the Wallises) owned a big place up in Connecticut, and they would take my children, and she, the madam, would do for my children just what she did for theirs.

> INTERVIEWER: What kinds of things do you think your children learned from that, from the time they spent with them?

> MRS. HUDSON: Well, I think what they learnt from them, to try to live a decent life themselves, and try to make the best out of their life and the best out of the education they had. So I think that's what they got from them.

> INTERVIEWER: What would you say you liked most about the work you did?

> MRS. HUDSON: Well what I liked most about it, the things that I weren't able to go to school to do for my children, I could kinda pattern from the families that I worked for, so that I could give my children the best of my abilities. I think that's the thing I got from them, 'though they couldn't become professors, they could be good in whatever they did.

The warm, personal relationship between the two families was based not only on the direct assistance which the Wallises gave Mrs. Hudson, but also on the ways in which she was able to utilize her position in their family to support and sustain her personal goals. Thus, we can understand why she saw work as an ability rather than a burden. Work was a means for attaining her goals; it provided her with the money she needed to be an independent person, and it exposed her and her children to "good" things—values and a style of life which she considered important. To some extent, Lena Hudson found the same things in her work that she found in her church: reinforcement for the standards which she held for her children and for herself.

Her ability to utilize her work experience in this way is an example of the active, self-determining approach she took to life. However, as her statement comparing the Wallises' goals for their children and for hers indicates, she was also aware of her social position and of the consequent limitations it placed on her abilities. She was self-determining, therefore, within limits.

At a point in the interview when she was describing the job she held as a governess with the Steuben family, she said: "You had to know your place." It is fair to argue that Lena Hudson not only knew her place in her role of servant in an employer's household, but also in the society at large. Her place was defined primarily by poverty and race. Yet in the interview, while she acknowledges the importance of these factors, she does not talk about them very much. She talks, for example, about not having the "means" to do for her children what the Wallises could do for theirs. And, in discussing the adjustments she had to make in her job as governess, she said:

> Well, I had to learn to take them, one thing; takin' bein' around White people all the time. I had to learn to be a good listener. Their conversation is not your conversation but you has to be there. . . . So, not bein' accustomed to a thing like that, you had to know your place.

In general, the tone of the interview is optimistic. It focuses upon her efforts to take advantage of the opportunities that were available to her, rather than despairing about the hardships she encountered.

Mrs. Hudson had talked about her children and her jobs for some time before she said anything about her husband. When she did mention him, she said:

> I haven't talked about him because—he was a good man, but not a family man. Sometime I knew where he was, and sometime I didn't. So, I found out what I had to do, I had to raise the family. I just forgot about him. When he came it was all right; and if he didn't come it was all right.

What did it mean to be a "good man but not a family man"? She continued:

When I came to New York I came to my husband, and the
conditions that he were living under. He was rooming, and part
of the time he was working and part of the time he wasn't. So
I just had to get out. I'd saw what I had to do and I saw what
kind of a man he was; he wasn't a man to stay on a job long.
Wasn't a mean man, was just, he came first, you know, and if
he felt like working he'd work and if he didn't, he didn't.
Raising a family you can't be like that, especially if you have
a little standard, the way you want to raise your family. So I
just forgot I had a husband, and raised my family.

Mr. Wilbur Hudson's lifestyle did not augment the standards which
Mrs. Hudson had made for herself and for her children. According to
her description of him, he did not strive to "be something" or set an
example for the children by "living a good life before them." As a
result, she chose to leave him. But her feelings about him were not as
cut-and-dried as these early statements imply. As the interview
continued and we began to develop greater rapport, she revealed more
of her feelings:

[I] lived with my sister until I got pregnant and I had a room.
My husband was with me then. I had a room and this lady
said, when the baby came you had to get another place to go,
because she didn't want any children in her house. So, as I
told you, my husband never had a job. I was spoken to, to be
a superintendent in an old White house (a building with elderly
White tenants). This was a cold water flat. So, I'd taken that,
and when the children came they were twins. So I stayed there
until I guess they might have been one or two years old. Then
my husband got an apartment and we were dispossessed from
there and I had to go out on my own. That was when relief
(welfare benefits) first come in. After he left they gave me
some relief and I was in an apartment. When I got all settled,
he wanted to come home. So I had to tell the investigator that
he wanted to come home. They let him come home, they gave
him a job with the WPA, and he worked there certain length
of time. He was taken' his lunch every day, goin' to work, and
he wasn't workin' at all. So I've had it, well I would say
pretty bad, but I was always able to make ends meet. So, he

completely walked away from home. Then I was put on relief for a certain length of time and I'd, well not all o' my life, but I've had it pretty tough see. I got a room with a lady in the basement with my four children and that time I was recommended by this lady to Community Service Society. The Community Society sent me to the Wallises. . . . I worked there and I began to make twenty-five dollars a week. I cut the relief off. Then I could take care of my house. And from then on I kept goin' and goin' and goin' till it got better and better.

This statement conveys some of the anger and frustration she experienced in her marriage. It indicates that her first reaction to their troubles was not to try to forget him but to try and hold the marriage together. She took him back several times, though not without resentment. Yet, the fact that she let him come home conveys her own recognition that as a young woman she had feelings, needs, and desires that could not be rigidly programmed. As she described it, almost every time he came back, during the seven years they were together, she got pregnant. And in spite of the problems, she maintained a strong sense of loyalty to him, taking him back into her home when he became seriously ill, after an almost forty-year separation. While her loyalty to him may seem somewhat surprising, it is totally consistent with her presentation of herself as a long-suffering, Christian woman, who forgave her enemies and expressed malice towards no one. Her understanding and acceptance of her husband's faults parallels the feelings she expressed towards some of her early, more exploitative employers. Although the statement ends on a note of optimism, displaying the self-determination which was characteristic of her conversation throughout the interview, she also concedes that her life was rough.

Wilbur Hudson appears to be his wife's life story in the same way he participated in her life—infrequently. Sometimes he's there, sometimes he's not; but at all times he's tangential to her struggle to raise, educate and mold the children. The support which she received for her goals and values about family life came primarily from her church and from the families for whom she worked. It is to these things which she attributes her children's good life. For herself, she admits:

I knew I had a family and had to take care of them, so I didn't
have much pleasure in those days—wasn't any pleasure to
have, no more than see that my children were coming up right.

It appears that when she gave up her hopes of sustaining the
marriage, she gave up her search for personal fulfillment with another
man or in a lively social life and directed most of her energies towards
rearing the children. Her participation in church, her involvement with
her jobs and the fact that she had "good" children made her life good.

What was Lena Hudson's relationship to her children as they were
growing up? In what ways did she interact with them and with her
employer's children? How did she discipline them and for what
reasons? The clearest sense of Mrs. Hudson's style of mothering can be
gleaned from her comments about the children of her employers. Her
discussion of these children reveals most about her manner of
interacting with children as well as her basic childrearing practices.
While initially appearing somewhat paradoxical, her emphasis upon
these matters in her conversation about the children of her employers
is understandable. After all, her responsibilities for the employer's
children centered on the day to day tasks of childcare. While with her
own children, she not only had to perform these daily activities but also
had responsibility for determining and supervising their overall direction
in life, a duty which, as has already been noted, she placed above all
others. On the whole, she characterized the rearing of her own children
in terms of life-goals and standards and the care of her employer's
children in terms of their interactions. To some extent, this difference
permitted her greater freedom and ease in relating to the employer's
children than it did with her own.

Regarding the Steuben children, she said:

They confided in me. . . . Yes, they did. Their mother said to
me she had to come to me to find out about the children. So
they'd confide in me, every little thing, they would come to
me. There was nothin', I was right down with them as they
were growing up in age, you know, they could talk to me
'bout different things, going with girls and what to expect and,
they just confided in me, more than my children did, in a way.
I been through all their education. They workin' hard and

asked me different things they wouldn't ask their mother because I was with them all the time, you see.

About her own children she said:

I could never say my own children and I didn't see eye to eye because I was right with them all the time, you see. They know my ways and what I would stand for, and they know to abide by what I said.

These two statements provide interesting contrasts and similarities. The comment about her own children stresses discipline while that about the Steuben children stresses communication, a difference which was consistent with her concerns as a parent for her own children's future and with her role as caretaker for her employer's children. Also, the use of discipline as a means of preparing children for a harsh and restrictive world was perhaps perceived as more relevant for her own children. For both sets of children, however, being "right down with them" was obviously something she considered to be an important part of mothering. We explored this issue in greater depth in relationship to Mrs. Steuben, a college professor.

Well, a person like that, just their career come ahead of their children. They can afford to have somebody stay home and raise 'em and still keep up a career. . . . It's good and sometime it's bad. Because when this last child was born, he and his mother could never see eye to eye. She's a very nice lady but she didn't have patience like the child thought she should have. You know you have to be 'round your children. She's a very good mother, but they just couldn't see eye to eye on some things. I think that is because the mother doesn't stay home with her child. I think she should stay home with the child. It'll understand you, and you'll understand it. Taking care of them, she seen that they had everything. She was with them at night, she wasn't a social butterfly. But you know when children grow up, they well, they just like to be around their mother, you know. Mother can really understand the child better. I would never say . . . my children and I didn't see eye to eye because I was right with them all the time, you see.

Mrs. Hudson's criticism of Mrs. Steuben is striking in light of the fact that *both* women worked and that *each* had a job which limited the time she could spend with her children. Clearly, in Mrs. Hudson's view, they worked for different reasons, reasons which she could understand but not fully accept. From Mrs. Hudson's perspective, Mrs. Steuben put her work ahead of her children and worked, essentially, for herself. She, on the other hand, saw herself as working for her children, putting them ahead of everything else. Nevertheless, her understanding of this issue went beyond these differences between them.

> The children would cling more to him than they would to the mother, because the father was very understanding about what the child wants to do when the mother would just say no. They'd go to their father and he was soft and would talk to them about it and explain to 'em and maybe he could do more with 'em like that. You do more with a child if you sit down and talk to it and get their understanding. You can do more with that child than you can with a child, if the child come and ask you a question, you said, No, you can't do it, you just can't do it. Now that child know Mama is not going to explain.

Patience and understanding are projected as characteristics which Mrs. Steuben lacked in relating to her children. Although Mrs. Hudson is not explicit, it appears that the priorities they set with regard to work and children are only one of the differences between the two women. Another is their style of mothering; cultural, class and other differences shaped the ways they interacted with their children when they were with them. Mrs. Hudson describes herself as patient and understanding of the child's perspective, even as a disciplinarian.

> I tried to live with my children, and I wasn't a parent that you'd be 'fraid of. You'd come to me whatever happens to you. Don't try to go to somebody else. And I used to tell them (the Steuben and Wallis children) the same thing. 'Cause I was their overseer. Whatever happens, let me know. Maybe something I can straighten out, you can't take care for yourself.

For Mrs. Hudson, mothering was fundamentally a way of relating to children that was not confined to the interaction between a mother and her natural-born children. Many components of this style, such as her efforts to talk openly and frankly with children about sex, drugs and other matters which concerned them, were transferable to all of the children whom she raised. And though she recognized that her relationship to the Wallis and Steuben children was based on the successful performance of her job, she talked about them as "my boys," stayed in touch with them, and remained vitally interested in their futures.

Jewell Prieleau

Jewell Prieleau migrated to New York in 1939, secured a job as a live-in housekeeper with the Lichtman family in 1945 and was still living there and working for them when interviewed in 1976. Her conversation about the 31 years she had spent on that job began and ended with the same complaint: their lack of consideration for her personal time.

> Well, the major thing in unfairness was holidays off. And you have no special time to get off at night. After you work for a family for a while they never think to ask you, "Would you mind serve dinner for us tonight, we having company?" They just says, "Well, we having company. Listen, Mrs. So-and-so is coming." You never know ahead of time. No matter what sort of plans you have, they plan right over you.

As her story unfolded, it became increasingly apparent that while this aspect of her relationship with the Lichtmans was the issue through which many of her dissatisfactions with her work and life were expressed, it was not just the lack of time that she was complaining about. Jewell Prieleau was angry about the inequities of that relationship and the factors of poverty and race which had so limited her life choices. Unlike Lena Hudson, she was very explicit about the harshness of her life and she openly acknowledged the social differences which accounted for that. In what began as a discussion of the people who lived in the Lichtman's apartment building on Fifth Avenue, she said:

They don't know nothing about a hard life. The only hard life
will come if they getting a divorce or going through a problem
with their children. But their husband has to provide for them
because they're not soft. And if they leave and they separate
for any reason or [are] divorced, they have to put the money
down. But we have no luck like that. We have to leave our
children; sometime leave the children alone. There's times
when I have to ask winos to look after my children. It was just
a terrible life and I really thank God that the children grow up
to be nice.

Jewell Prieleau's language is an indicator of her sense of social
location. She used the terms "we" and "they" to express the distinction
between people like herself and people like the Lichtmans. I interpreted
"we" to refer to oppressed people, particularly poor and/or Black
women like herself, and "they" to refer to the exploiters who were rich
and/or White people. She repeated these categories throughout the
interview, expressing a keen awareness of her social position and of the
differences between her own family and her employer's.

Mrs. Prieleau did have a hard life and the limitations imposed by
the structure of a live-in job appear to have only intensified her
problems. Nevertheless, she took this job and stayed there because it
seemed to provide security, a steady income, and the best means of
helping her family.

The war was going on when I came to the Lichtmans and they
told me if I stayed with them I would never miss my pay. You
know the girls was very hard to get in those days. A lot of the
people just leave and went to work on other jobs. After the
war, most of them came back to domestic work.

Since she had done domestic work for almost sixteen years in her
hometown of Beaufort, South Carolina before coming North, we can
reasonably assume that she would have understood that a live-in job in
New York would have had the advantage of increasing her ability to
assist her family financially and the disadvantage of giving her little
time to share with them. Despite the drawbacks, she came, and
described her reasons for doing so as follows:

Well, you know, it's funny, whenever you have trouble in the South you always feel, "Well, I go to New York and I work for a while." You just feel that it's something here. "I'll go to New York and I'll work for a while and I'll have money for myself and I'll send money for my daughter or son or whatever."

So, when she and her husband began to have problems, she decided to move to New York, leaving her two-year-old daughter, Joella, with her husband's mother who had said: "Listen, your trouble is my trouble and I'll take the baby and raise her." She made trips home

. . . at least once every year. Once in a while, twice. In case of emergency, if my mother was sick, I would always go to see her and we (she and Joella) stay in touch with each other.

. . . And after I came here, I said, I'll stay two years or maybe a year and I just stayed and stayed and it went by very fast.

Her decision to come North and work turned out to be gravely ironic. While she was able to help her family financially, she was not available to participate daily in her daughter's development. It was not until Joella had become fifteen and her grandmother had died that she came to New York to live and to begin spending time with her mother. Even then, their time together was limited by the constraints of Mrs. Prieleau's job. One such constraint was in living arrangements. Mrs. Prieleau lived in the Lichtman's apartment. She could not take Joella to stay with her there and did not choose to move out of the Lichtman household. So, Joella stayed in a room in Harlem by herself and her mother visited her whenever she could:

When Joella came to New York she was fifteen, but she wanted me to spend a little time with her sometimes. Of course, holidays and days like that the Lichtmans want for themselves with they family. They would never think of saying, "Well, we'll have company this New Year's, later next New Year's we'll let you go to your family." They never think anything like that. They always feel they come first.

There was times when she (Joella) would spend the night here.
But of course, if they knew, they would object to that and
think that you know, this room is too small or what have you.
Still, there was just times when I let her stay here.

The arrangements which Mrs. Prieleau made for Joella at this time
had a major effect on the family's later development. Thus, it is
important that we attempt to understand why she selected this course of
action. By constructing a hypothetical model based on her retrospective
statements about that period, we can perhaps review the possible options
she may have had and the ways in which she might have viewed them.

A first such option would have been moving Joella into the
Lichtman household with her and creating a job for her there. However,
Mrs. Prieleau's statement above makes it fairly clear that this was not
a viable alternative. As she said in describing Mrs. Lichtman:

She is a social worker and she understands a lot of things but
they just don't want you to bring trouble into their homes.

Joella's arrival when she was fifteen, without perceptible skills that
would enhance the family life of the Lichtmans, must have seemed
troublesome at best, and at the least, inconvenient. Accommodations for
the child of a trusted employee on a big estate in Connecticut might not
have been hard to come by. In New York City, however, apartment
space has always been at a premium and Joella, after all, was not really
their concern.

A second option might have been for Mrs. Prieleau to keep the job
but move and set up housekeeping with Joella. Even if the Lichtmans
were agreeable to it—and Mrs. Prieleau gives no indication that she
thought they would be—this strategy would have had limitations. Most
importantly, food, rent and incidentals associated with the upkeep of an
apartment or of a larger room would have decreased the amount of
money that could be put aside to help others in her family. In addition,
she gives us no reason to believe that the responsibilities of her job
would have decreased appreciably. Had they remained the same, she
would not have been able to increase the time she could spend with
Joella even if they had been living together.

Then there was the option of leaving the job entirely and taking
another job in housework or in some other kind of work that could have

given her more time with her child. But, as pointed out above, domestic work was all she knew and in her occupation a worker achieved economic stability by working for an economically stable family. The Lichtmans were such a family. In statements quoted above Mrs. Prieleau made it clear that the security and stability provided by this job were its fundamental advantage.

> Once you work for a family for a while they do pay your doctor's bill, which when they pay their income tax they get it off. And I know if something turn up and I wouldn't have my rent money or am sick for a while, I feel for sure they would give me something.

It is unlikely, therefore, that she would think that she could find a situation that would have been much better.

Finally, there was Joella herself who, at age fifteen to a mother who did not know her well, might have appeared to be more like an adult than a child in need of supervision. Mrs. Prieleau had not experienced adolescence herself. At a very young age she was out working and contributing to her family's support.

> When I was eight years old I decided I wanted a job and I just got up early in the morning and I would go from house to house and ring doorbells and ask for jobs and I would get it. I think I really wanted to work because, see, in a big family like that, they was able to feed you, but you had to earn your shoes. . . . They couldn't buy shoes although shoes was very cheap at that time. So we had to wait a while. And I always would rather my mother give it to the younger children and I would earn my way.

Although the ideo-typical constructions that were developed above cannot specify reasons why Mrs. Prieleau settled on one particular living arrangement for Joella, they do provide some insight into the complexities of the interaction between work and family. The nature of her work and of the job opportunities available to her shaped the field of options which she had to consider. It is likely that she saw no alternatives to household work and that within the occupation the job she was holding was attractive enough to make personal sacrifices seem worthwhile. It is within these constraints—which are perhaps more apparent in retrospect than they were at that time—that Jewell Prieleau made choices based on her goals for her *entire* family, of which Joella was only one member. In this sense, work was primarily a means to an end rather than an end in itself; and family commitments which extended beyond the nuclear unit were one of the major reasons for doing this kind of work.

Her choice, however, resulted in Joella's being left alone most of the time. So it is not surprising that, after being in New York for less than a year, Joella married. Reflecting on the marriage, Mrs. Prieleau said:

> I shouldn't have let her get married so early but I couldn't be there to watch her. She met someone that was ten years older than she was. And you know, it was a little nicer that she should get married than be left alone.

Marriage offered the promise of protection and companionship for Joella as well as providing someone, a man ten years older and raised in their hometown, to "watch" her. Perhaps she expected the husband to replace, in some ways, the recently deceased grandmother and to fulfill a role that she herself never accepted. But the promise was not realized. The marriage failed.

> They was constantly moving. They was dispossessed. She was looking for a place most of the time, you know. So finally she ran into a terrible nervous breakdown. So after I serve breakfast in the morning I could clean up right quick and go and help her look for a place. I had to borrow money to pay the deposit. Places were hard to find and I had three small grandchildren. After that my daughter started drinking so much from her problems. Child that she was, brought up without the mother and father together, no matter what happens there's something missing and that child has that defect, if you can call it that.

At the point at which she began to talk about the failure of Joella's marriage, Mrs. Prieleau also shifts her discussion of familial concerns from her family of orientation to her family of procreation. She described herself as taking over a major portion of the care of the grandchildren as well as caring for her daughter. It is at this point that her attitude towards the job appears to have become less acquiescent and more manipulative.

> There was times when I kept my grandchildren here (at the job) you know. My daughter and her husband had trouble and they separated and I kept my grandchildren here because I didn't want to just leave them with her and she was upset most of the time. I got up early in the morning and send them off to school from here. After school I would pick them up in a taxi and bring them . . . and they were nice children, they would sit back there and behave nicely. Then when she (Mrs. Lichtman) would find that they was here, she would fuss a bit; "Where's your daughter, where's your son-in-law" you know, things like that.

While she did not keep her grandchildren at the Lichtman home on a regular basis or over a long period of time, she gives the impression that she devoted more time to them than she had Joella. By this time, however, she had been working for the Lichtman family for close to fifteen years, their children were older and did not need her full-time, her position in their household was more secure.

In addition to these changes in her life, there were emotional ones. She obviously felt guilty about neglecting Joella when she was growing up.

> Well, I think what I should have done was to bring her here with me and stay with her. Although it would have been hard, we would have had that love for each other. That's my biggest disappointment and I also would have liked to stayed with my husband until she got herself of age. And I shouldn't have let her get married so early.

This is the irony of Mrs. Prieleau's story: the choices which she made in order to support and protect some members of her family had the opposite results for others.

Upon examination of her choices and the range of probable alternatives, it becomes increasingly apparent that, while the choices were personal, they were also socially situated and occurred within the constraints of being poor, black, and female. Mrs. Prieleau made it quite clear that she understood the concrete meaning of these limitations in her life. At several points in the interview she talked about how hard it was for her without a husband and how she wished for a strong man. In fact, one of the things she admired most in the Lichtman family was Mr. Lichtman's performance of his role as husband and father.

> Well, she (Mrs. L) have a very nice husband and I would like somebody like that. They have so much in common with each other and they get along nicely together. I would like something like that. . . . He was what one would call a family man. That's what I would like. Nothing comes in front of his family, no matter where he is at. . . . A White man—you know I'm not saying it the way I should—but they always think more of their family. My husband would never say, "Well, you're working too late on that job I would rather you quit and get another job or look for something." He wouldn't say that. When we go to work like that, they want you have to pay half the expense and then they take their half of the money and do something else with it. And more and more men are spoiled like that. Now I don't know everybody but quite a few of them they really especially want a hard working woman.

Initially, I was somewhat surprised that a woman who had expressed such a strong sense of social identity and awareness of the social conditions which had influenced her life-choices, did not readily acknowledge the fact that Black men were victims of similar circumstances. In a word, I was surprised that she expressed resentment towards the men rather than the conditions which resulted in their lack of economic security. In thinking about what she said, however, I was reminded that the failure of her first and second marriages and that of her daughter were very *personal* experiences, thought of in personal, not societal terms. While she did not share many details about the basis for any of these break-ups, the anguish in her voice as she talked clearly indicated that they had hurt her deeply. Thus, I came to understand that the statements which she made about Black men were personal statements; reflections of her lonely struggle to survive and support her family without the kind of help she had hoped for from any of the men whom she had loved. Jane Halowell Coles and Robert Coles found a similar pattern among the women they interviewed and explained it thus:

> For many of the women we have come to know these past decades, the enemy is a given social order, yes; an economic system yes; but also and quite distinctly—or as George Eliot might want us to say, quite definitely—a certain number of men. Not just *a* man; rarely have we met a woman who is unwilling to connect the serious and demeaning hurts of her life with the behavior of more than one person. Yet, when an unhappy and complaining (or protesting) woman begins to move her attention from the individual or idiosyncratic to a broader arc of humanity, a certain psychological "indefiniteness" will inevitably be the price, a sense of frustration and perplexity: where to begin with one's resentment and moral, personal outrage? Put differently, a specific denunciation brings more immediate satisfaction.[1]

In the same way that disparities of economic and social resources shaped the kind of support men could provide for their women, they influenced parental ability to care for and protect the children. In answer to the question: "What about the way she (Mrs. Lichtman) raised her children did you like?" Mrs. Prieleau replied:

> Whenever they come home from school they had to come right home. She would not have her children go to anyone's house to sleep unless she know the people. She was very careful with they friends, and she see that her children go to a nice camp. She always keep her children in a nice school. She dress them nice (of course, you can't tell now the way children dress), but her children always dress nice and she always had people to keep their clothes nice. There was always someone here with her children. Whenever [the daughter] was going to music school or any place, I had to take her in a taxi. Whenever she finish, she had to be picked up. I had to go get her. Her children was never leaved to run around New York. When they come from school in the spring, when it was light outside, they played right in front of the door. They was never allowed to go

in the park or anything. Her children was well protected at all
times.

The fact that the Lichtman children were "well protected at all times"
is the outstanding theme of this entire statement and reflects one of the
most poignant variations between the two families.

The Lichtmans were able to purchase the kind and range of services
that insured their children's well-being. Mrs. Prieleau was one of those
services; camp, music lessons, a nice school, nice clothing and carefully
selected friends were others. She, on the other hand, relied heavily on
God, credit, and propitious circumstances to help her provide for her
children. Contrast her description of the Lichtman children's lifestyles
with that of her grandson.

> I have a grandson who's 20 years old. He's exceptionally nice.
> He go to college in Brooklyn; one of those low budget
> colleges. He was always a smart boy. So the last move we
> made, we moved out to Brooklyn. And he met some nice
> White boys out there because at that time they was a lot of
> White people used to live out there. And he was very friendly
> with the boys and I thought that helped to make him a nice
> boy too, you know. . . . Now my grandson was growing up, he
> just grow right up in a pack of dope addict and every day I
> was just looking to see something like that. But I would call
> on the elders of the church to pray. I would pray and
> everytime I know of a strong person in my church that really
> pray, I tell him to pray. And, I'm still praying.

In this statement, she attributes events to a combination of self-
determination, choosing to move to Brooklyn, the right associates and
peers, and religious faith. The "pack of dope addict" [*sic*] characterize
the original community as a rough one and imply that she felt she had
little personal control over what could happen to her grandson in that
situation. The best option, therefore, was to move away and they moved
into a neighborhood in which "at that time . . . a lot of White people
used to live." This phrase, in itself, tells us a lot about the nature of
their move. It tells us that they moved from a deteriorating
neighborhood into one that was changing from White to Black. At the
same time they moved in, however, the new neighborhood still had

many of the advantages that remain in such communities until sometime after it has become all Black: good schools, sound housing, and reliable services. The "nice White boys" who populated this community provided a stark contrast to the "pack of dope addict" in their old neighborhood and indicated what the move meant to her. In her description of the old community, she emphasized prayer as the key to helping her grandson avoid the negative influences which surrounded him; in the new one, the community itself was depicted as being more supportive of her goals and values.

Nevertheless, church and a strong belief in God were fundamental aspects of childrearing for the grandchildren.

> Well, the children would go to Sunday School in the morning and they would teach them the Bible. They really teach children the way of holiness. Now a child would know when they grow up not to take knives in their pocket, depend on God, that God would take care of them, to love each other, not to abuse one another—hurt their feeling, or just take up an iron plate and smash it across your head. If a person is God-fearing that person really is a well-behaved person. I think that had a lot to do for the children. They know how to sing. They know how to pray.

Jewell Prieleau describes religious teachings that are pragmatic, focused upon the realities she could have expected the children to encounter in their original neighborhood. Like Lena Hudson, she used the church to provide protection and values for the children, oftentimes in the parent's absence. Mrs. Hudson emphasized the presence of the institution itself, the activities and programs which kept the children busy and off the streets. Mrs. Prieleau emphasized the teachings.

While moving to a new neighborhood and sending the children to church were the strategies she employed to aid in the children's development, there are several situations in which she was unable to protect them. One such incident resulted in the death of one of her grandchildren.

> We leave her with someone and the person let her eat lead poison so she died and she (the woman the child was left with) never did admit it. But the doctors said that's what it was.

Another was the death of her infant son some 25 years earlier in the South.

> I had a child shortly after I was married, a little boy. And after
> that Joella in '37. . . . He died. He was born with the cord
> around his neck. The doctor wasn't there and he just choked
> to death. I was home. At that time the doctors didn't come to
> the house, you have a midwife. But I was home and I called
> the doctor and the doctor came and he said, "Oh no, you're not
> going to have this baby 'fore tomorrow or next week
> sometime." You know at that time they cared very little about
> you. They just didn't care. So he wasn't gone two hours before
> the baby was born. And then I called back. So he come when
> he got good and ready. Almost the same thing happened when
> Joella was born. She was born like that at home and she had
> a very, very big navel because the doctor didn't take care of
> her.

In light of the strategies she used to protect her children and the situations in which she was unable to protect them, it is quite clear why Jewell Prieleau admired and envied the Lichtmans' ability to both protect their children and give them many of the "nicer" things in life. It is also clear why she resented them. Where she could, she tried to do similar things for her grandchildren. Moving to Brooklyn was one effort to get better schools and a nice, safe community. She also prided herself on getting them nice clothes.

> I went to three nice department stores and I opened up credit
> for them so that I could send them to school looking nice.

And, when she kept the children at the Lichtmans, she did for them what she had done for the Lichtman children: "After school," she said, "I would pick them up in a taxi and bring them here."

Much of the discussion above indicates her admiration for and identification with certain aspects of the Lichtmans' lifestyle, yet her sense of social placement was like a rudder, continuously helping her maintain a balanced view of her job and her employers. When asked: "Do you think they (the Lichtmans) see you like a member of the family or do they see you as —?" she replied:

Well, they tell you that. But of course you have the feeling, because you know that if something goes wrong, something they didn't like, how fast they would let you go. But people would come in and say, "Oh well, this is Jewell. She was here with me for twenty-five or thirty years." And the person would say, "Oh, then she is a part of the family." She would say, "Well, you bet!" But you know, I don't feel that way because you work with a family, sometime they would come in and say, "Let's sit down and have a cup of coffee together." They would lay in bed and call you and you stand by the door and talk to them until you almost drop. They never ask you to sit on the bed or anything. Not only her, they all like that you know. . . . But there is just a feeling between you that you know you can cover up for years and years, but that feeling in both parties is there. . . . They nice and they treat me nice like a person would treat a maid. But you know they wouldn't go out of their way so much. But they really treat me nice.

Like Lena Hudson, Jewell Prieleau "knew her place" as a maid in the Lichtman household and though she openly expressed greater resentment toward these inequities, her basic philosophy was reminiscent of Mrs. Hudson's. At the end of the statement where she compares the type of "hard life" that people like the Lichtmans experienced with her own life, she said:

. . . But the main things to look at in life is try not to be sorry for yourself and you just have to feel sometime that you're going through hard places. I mean, you know you'll get good out of it sooner or later. Because now things begin to shape up kind of nice for me. So I thank God, I didn't lose my mind.

Her belief that good could come out of the bleakest situation is probably the thing which kept her from losing her mind and from being overcome by resentment towards those who had more than she did. Nevertheless, she did recognize and resent these inequities. Her description of the Lichtmans' lifestyle provides an example of the way she balanced these feelings.

MRS. PRIELEAU: But these people around here do nothing but dress. They have nothing to do but to dress. And they go to

the beauty parlor, do their nails; and they dress up nice and
walk around Madison Avenue you know and stop in a swanky
restaurant and eat and just look in the stores.

INTERVIEWER: How do you feel about that? Does it bother you?

MRS. PRIELEAU: You know when I was younger I thought
things like that but as I got older I begin to feel well, maybe
that's the way it is so there's nothing you can do about it. . . .
Some people are blessed and have money and they just don't
do anything.

In the final analysis, she created an explanation for these
inequalities which relied on fate. Nevertheless, it is perhaps her
unwilling acceptance of it, her resentment and her sense of social
identity that helped her to overcome total despair and immobilization.
Another one of her weapons was her sense of humor. She exhibited a
keen sense of satire and her descriptions of the Lichtmans and their
friends frequently employed this form of social criticism. For example:

I've never seen anything like it. They like flocks of birds.
They all flock down to Florida now and from March they
come back to New York. And they see each other, every day
on the beach. They come back to New York and they want to
sit and eat everyday. And they invite each other. They go from
house to house, you know. And they just like to sit down and
say, "Oh Mr. and Mrs. Green was here last night, Mr. and
Mrs. Brown was here the night before." People on Park
Avenue and Fifth Avenue, they have a lot of company because
they call that highly sociable you know. The more company,
the more liquor is served and then they like to come in with
beautiful evening gowns on in the evening and they stand.

The feelings which she expresses towards people living on Park and
Fifth Avenues, while humorous, also convey her disdain for many
aspects of their lives. When asked: "If you were to switch places with
Mrs. Lichtman . . . what would you do differently in terms of someone
who worked for you?" she replied:

Oh, I wouldn't like switching place with her because I have noticed that although people are very very rich and they have everything, they very unhappy underneath and sometimes it shows on them. I don't want to be unhappy. I don't know I just don't admire them because I've noticed they come to dinner and they complain about hangnails and little things like that. And they just get to themselves and cry. And do you know that half these rich people around here they wind up on all sorts of things. . . . Now there's women in this building here, they husbands are big _____ firms and they have racing stable and everything and there's no, really—there's no relief twenty-four hours a day. They change their clothes, they going out the door and they see the sun and they turn back; they put on a fur. But deep underneath they not happy. I've never seen just an actually happy person and I know nine out of ten times they're all going to a psychiatrist. This way, I live half poor, I go without a meal once and a while. So I just pray and I get my stomach full.

Her awareness of the anomalies of her employer's life helped her maintain a sense of determination and self-respect in the face of glaring economic inequities. It also helped her explain her own deprivation:

I don't think I would want to change, but I would like to live differently. I would like to have my own nice little apartment with my husband and have my grandchildren for dinner and my daughter and just live comfortable, but I would always want to work. I wouldn't say domestic, but I would always want to work. But if I was to change life with them, I would like to have just a little bit of they money, that's all.

Like Lena Hudson, Jewell Prieleau's goals appear quite modest. However, when we consider the problems she confronted in her life, we know that the effort to attain these things was and is a continuing struggle. The fact that she wants so little in the face of so much provides the most poignant statement possible about the interaction of her values with those of the Lichtmans. She expressed greatest admiration for the strong husband/father role as Mr. Lichtman performed it, for Mrs. Lichtman's ability to protect and shelter her children, and for the goods and services their money permitted them to purchase.

At the same time she expressed disdain for many aspects of their lives, specifically the idleness of the women. This panoply of feelings and opinions is directly related to the different social and economic positions of the two families. It is understandable that daily participation in such discrepant conditions of life would create conflict. Thus, like all oppressed people, she both admired and disdained those who benefited from her oppression.[2]

Opallou Tucker

Unlike either Lena Hudson or Jewell Prieleau, Opallou Tucker did not work full-time for one family over many years. She did days work, "a day here and a day there," for a number of different people throughout her years as a household worker. Sometimes she worked on catering jobs, sometimes she did cooking or general cleaning, and for many years she worked as the laundress in a large household. She worked while she and her husband were raising their four children, a responsibility which she proudly characterized as being equally shared between the two of them. At the beginning of the interview, she talked about her work and her family:

> We had two children and when my son was about nine months old, I felt the need of going back to work. So a friend of mine kept the children during the day and I did what was known as days work; a day here and a day there. By the time the third child was coming along, I began to do just straight out cooking and serving, catering, and work with someone who was doing catering—when they had the job I went along with them. I continued doing that through the four children and all along while the children were going to school. I had no difficulty because I lived in a very nice neighborhood . . . and everybody there, White and Black were all working. In fact, there was only one house of Black anyway and we were the only ones that had any children. All the White women were going out to work and I was going out to work and the children watched each other, more or less. The bigger ones were big enough to watch the two little ones. They went to school within three

blocks of the house and they came home for lunch. People talk about children with keys around their necks; they had their keys but they never got into anything. They never had any difficulty. They went in, had their lunch and the older ones locked the door and they went back to school. If I was home in the morning, I wasn't home in the evening, their father always was home by six o'clock. I had nothing to worry about. I could always call home and he was there. So, that's the way it continued to be throughout the bringing up of the children.

The notion that children of working mothers were particularly vulnerable to the evils of city streets was presented by both Mrs. Hudson and Mrs. Prieleau. It reflects not only the realities of the communities in which they lived but a general social concern of the period that focused upon the relationship of working mothers to juvenile delinquency. The image of a young child with a "latchkey" around his or her neck, gradually getting into more and more trouble, was a dominant one in the '40s. It is not surprising, therefore, that both Mrs. Hudson and Mrs. Tucker should evoke it in discussing their relative success in raising their children.

Mrs. Tucker identified the neighborhood, a friend and, above all, her husband as her major sources of support in working outside the home.

The neighborhood we lived in—nobody was going to let your child stay at their house after dark. We didn't have to worry about that because most of them were middle income Whites and a few of them were poor White, but they weren't straggly and poor. And you'd go to Mary Jane's house, it's all right as long as Mama knows you're there. We all go to the same churches and the same schools and all that sort of stuff.

Her characterization of the community is noteworthy for its racial and socio-economic make-up as well as its shared communal activities. In this brief statement, she conveys a sense of the neighborhood as more than a street inhabited by an assortment of unassociated individuals who lived in apartments connected only by a common wall. It is depicted as a community—a place where people shared some of the important aspects of their lives, worshipping together, learning together, and raising their children together. Whether or not her neighbors could be formally classified as middle class is less important than the fact that the image they created in her mind was of hard-working people who shared some of the values she associated with middle class life, if not all of its rewards. The fact that even the poor folks were not "straggly," an expression which I interpret as meaning that they were not dirty, unkempt, immoral or uncouth by her standards, all reinforce the notion that this was a nice, decent neighborhood. In addition, she characterizes the neighborhood as a White neighborhood, a fact which, in her opinion, explains many of its "nicer" qualities. In the earlier discussion of Mrs. Prieleau's move to Brooklyn, some of the things that a White neighborhood represents in a racist society were identified. Those things included sound housing, good schools, and a safe environment in which to raise one's children—all indicators of upward mobility for a low-income Black family. It is clear that the churches, schools, and general community life represent what both Mrs. Prieleau and Mrs. Tucker associate with middle class status.

While the neighborhood provided one source of support, friends provided another. However, friends and kin were far less important for Mrs. Tucker or Mrs. Prieleau. Despite her mention of the friend who kept the two youngest children when she first returned to work, Mrs. Tucker does not refer to any other people, either friends or members of the extended kinship network, in discussing the raising of her children. When asked, "Were there any other people that you talked with about the children—what to do—or people who came by and babysat sometimes or something like that?" she replied:

> I never felt that anybody could take care of my children as well as I—the father and I, and I never asked anybody's advice about what to do for them, not even now. We never allowed anybody else to tell them what to do, because two or three different families can't bring up one set of children. It confuses them. That's my idea about it . . . that's the way we work in our household. . . . Those children never spent a night away from me except when I was in the hospital giving birth to another one. We kept our children together. There's no such thing as the grandmother raise part of the time or nothing of that sort. They were with the mother and father.

Mrs. Tucker's total commitment to and belief in the virtues of an isolated nuclear family are clearly communicated in these statements. The children were seen as solely her and her husband's responsibility and the two of them shared the duties of caring for them, occasionally putting older children in charge of the younger ones when neither parent was around. The image that she presents here and throughout the interview is of a family unit that is largely self-contained and self-sufficient. In fact, in talking about her family, she rarely referred to anyone other than her husband and the children. She mentions that she had sisters in the South whom she visited every couple of years and that she had had a pleasant childhood. Aside from that, however, she said little else about the family in which she was raised and nothing at all about her husband's kinfolk. It is as if marriage represented a break between her family of orientation and her family of procreation; a break which she implicitly identifies below:

> I had a good life and a fairly decent education. But education is one thing and food is another, and lodging. When I found out that you couldn't get food and lodging just by sitting around, then I went to work. I could very well have gone back home before I married, but after I married I would have never thought of going home and dragging a man home on my father. So I stayed here. And my husband of course wasn't the type of person that would have lived on anybody either, so we made our own life and brought our children up.

The possibilities for making her own life were enhanced and nurtured in the context of a marriage and family which she characterized as:

> A perfect family, a perfect marriage. We were well suited for each other, each one had his own mind and neither one tried to intrude on the other one's thoughts or privacy.

In her opinion her husband's participation in childcare activities was an outstanding component of their relationship. He also provided the most important and consistent support for her work outside the home. In reply to the question, "What kinds of things did your husband do in terms of the childrearing . . .?" she said:

Everything, everything! He would wash for the baby, iron for
the baby, bathe the children and at nights Mama was never
called when you had to get up and go to the bathroom. Daddy
put the light on. He always said, you had them in the daytime
when they were small, I'll take care of them at night. And I
didn't know what it was to diaper a baby, not even the little
baby. He got up and warmed the baby's bottle, gave the bottle,
changed the baby's pants, put the baby back in bed.

In addition to these caretaking tasks, James Tucker was very much
involved in his children's education. Education was viewed as the
means to a better life, specifically to what she termed "better" jobs than
those she had held. In fact, she was adamantly opposed to having her
children work "in service," and characterized this push towards
educational achievement as a major family activity.

Just made them go to school and mind their lessons so they'd
be able to get something else (other than domestic work) when
they got to the place where they could get something, that's
all. Studying was a very, very vital thing in our household.
Before you went to school you got your alphabet and from the
time you first started to go to school you learned your
multiplication tables. Their father was an excellent
mathematician and he saw to it from the very beginning that
you learned these multiplication tables or you got the belt.

According to Mrs. Tucker, Mr. Tucker did most of the "at home"
teaching. She said:

Well, he did more of that than I did. I let him have that job
because I had other things to do around the household and
when he was home from work in the evenings and Saturdays
and all that kind of stuff, he saw to it that they learned those
things. We got them to the place where studying wasn't
something that they dreaded so we had no difficulty.

Opallou Tucker portrays her husband as a committed and involved
father, a thoughtful and considerate husband, and a consistent provider
for his family. She gives the impression that she could always rely on

him to share the duties of keeping a house and caring for children, and she, in turn, shared the responsibilities of providing for the family. I suspect that this perception of their relationship and of its influence on all aspects of their lives provides an important explanation of her statement: "I wasn't handicapped by going out to work at all." Her children were not handicapped from lack of care or parental supervision and she was not handicapped in the job market by being the sole support of her family. Her family arrangements permitted her flexibility in choosing and maintaining jobs. Mrs. Tucker was more explicitly upwardly mobile than either Lena Hudson or Jewell Prieleau. She identified herself as middle class through her description of her neighborhood, her family life, and her jobs. Unlike either of the other two women, she spoke with a kind of autonomy and self-determination bordering on bravado about the ways in which she selected her jobs. And she firmly maintained throughout the interview that she had never had any problems with any of them.

> Just before I got married I started to doing housework and its no different from doing your own housework. If you work for somebody who's decent, which I've always done, because I would never think of working—not even now whatever type of work I do—I'd never work for anyone who was impossible. And I have an even temper, I believe, and I would work for no one who didn't have an even temper. So consequently, I never had any difficulty all through the years . . . .

Opallou Tucker conveys the impression that she did not have any problems because she did not allow them and because she carefully selected the type of work she would do as well as the kind of people who would be her employers.

> You see, most—as I say—my jobs I went on when I got ready. If it wasn't convenient for me or something happened that I couldn't do it today, I could do it tomorrow and that's one of the reasons why I never took a straightout cook's job, because if you're cooking, you've got to be there, but sewing or laundry or something of that sort, you go when you get ready and your pay is portal to portal. When you walk in your pay starts, when you walk out it ends.

She also had a strong opinion about working in a household with children.

> [A friend] . . . asked me if I would like to go and do this work
> for this woman, get the dinner for her that day. I said, "Sure,"
> because as I say, money was at a premium. So I went in and
> I said to myself, I wasn't going back anymore because that
> woman had a child. Which I had nothing against children, but
> I figured I had children at home. I didn't need to bother
> around them.

It is not clear from her conversation why she objected so strongly to working for someone who had children. We can only surmise that she perhaps saw it like she saw the "cook's job," ultimately requiring more of her personal time and energy than she wished to give. It is clear from examining both Mrs. Hudson's and Mrs. Prieleau's life stories that working for families with children could require a considerable investment of time and energy. In Mrs. Prieleau's case, this was compounded by the fact that she lived in. But even Mrs. Hudson, who did not live-in, gave the impression that she invested a lot of emotional energy in her employer's children. This resulted, in part, from her decision to partially intermingle her own family life with that of her employer's. Mrs. Tucker, however, did the exact opposite. She appears to have been unwilling to build emotional or personal bridges between her work and her family. She chose, instead, to devote all of her maternal time and energy to her own children and never became a surrogate mother, as did some of the participants of this study.[3] It has already been pointed out that she saw herself and her husband as making their "own life," and that she valued the isolated nuclear family. Part of this isolation could reasonably be expressed in the separation of work and family roles. So, even though she ultimately took the job with the child and stayed there for twenty-seven years, her duties as a laundress did not require her direct participation in caring for her employer's daughter. Although she spoke about the girl with warmth and even had a framed photograph of her in the living room, there is no sense that their relationship had any of the "surrogate" mother qualities that are discussed in Lena Hudson's case. Having a husband with full-time, stable employment was a major source of stability for the family and appears to be an important factor distinguishing the relationship of work and family for Mrs. Tucker from that of either Lena Hudson or Jewell Prieleau.

Opallou Tucker attributed her lack of problems in domestic jobs to two interacting influences: the type of people for whom she worked and the way in which she comported herself. She said:

> I was treated like I wanted to be treated, like a human being. I realized I was a servant in the household. When they asked me to do something—and I never had the misfortune of being asked to do anything that was degrading—when they asked me to do a job, if it happened to be a job that I went there to do, I would do it. I was always treated decently. No one ever tried to run over me. As I say, I am not the type you can run over anyway, really. They treat you, the ones I've been around, like you act. If you act intelligent, you're treated intelligent. . . . A lot of times people don't know their station in certain places. We all have a station whether it's in private life, public life, or on the job, we have a station. If we maintain our station, we're all right.

This statement conveys the notion that, to some extent, people are treated in direct response to the way they present themselves; those who carry themselves with dignity and intelligence receive that treatment in return. At the same time, however, she points out that she had good fortune and that she knew her station—a station which has few attributes of dignity associated with it. Knowing one's place, that is, accepting the fact that one is a servant with all that that entails, is apparently a key element in surviving as a domestic worker. All three women talked about it and each sought to create, through negotiation with the employer, a niche for themselves that permitted a certain amount of dignity within a subservient role.

In the interview, Mrs. Tucker sought to upgrade the role through emphasizing the caliber of people who did domestic work, the wealth and importance of her employers, the opportunities for learning on the job, her own middle class aspirations, and her personal sense of pride and dignity. She expressed very strong feelings about the inherent value of work, a value which gave household work greater meaning for her. She continued:

In the beginning when God created man, man was supposed to work. He was supposed to earn his bread by the sweat of his brow and he wasn't supposed to grovel in the dirt of course. I never encountered any difficulties about working. As the Campfire group has it, the Campfire Leaders, are supposed to glorify work and dignity. I think if we stop this business of certain people getting up saying this task is menial, I think we'd have much more—many more people working that sitting around expecting to get gratuities.

Like many of the women in this study, Mrs. Tucker felt called upon to defend her work. The defense she presents, however, is an ambivalent one, ambivalent because it acknowledges both the stigma attached to the occupation and her own contrasting feelings of dignity and self-worth. Her defense is both negative and positive. It is negative where she accepts the notion that domestic work is menial and argues that it is better to do menial work than none at all. It is positive in her notion that all work has dignity and there is therefore no such thing as a menial task. Both poles are present in the statements above and stand side by side throughout her discussion of the occupation.

Because she was ambivalent about her work, Mrs. Tucker's desire not have her children employed in domestic service was not unexpected. She said this, perhaps, because in contrast to one woman whom she knew to be training her daughter in catering work, she adamantly refused to even consider this option. In light of this, the stress which she and her husband placed on the education of their children takes on even greater importance. Mrs. Tucker gives the impression that she was a serious observer of social change. Thus, as she became aware of the expanding opportunities for Black people, she sought to ensure that her children were prepared to take advantage of them.

In the more positive aspects of her defense of the work, she stressed those things in her experience which she saw as symbolic of more prestigious occupations. These included education, wealth, power, and social status. For example, she talked at length about what she referred to as "misnomers" about all domestic workers being "ignorant and unlettered" people. She told stories of college graduates who did domestic work because there were no other jobs available for Black people at that time. In addition, she pointed out the opportunities for growth that could be experienced in domestic service. She said:

. . . Just because you're not working in a different type of work doesn't mean that you have to stop growing as far as your mind is concerned, as far as your knowledge, because you can continue to grow when you come home from what you're doing, and not only that. When you're thrown in with different people, you learn different things from the different nationalities, the people that you work with. Also you have the opportunity if you worked in the right environment of meeting people and coming in contact with some of the world's biggest people, men and women.

In her opinion, the right environment in which to work was a wealthy one.

So you see, I have never, as I say, worked for the poor class. I don't—this is an awful thing to say seeing as how I'm poor myself, but I don't particularly care to even associate with too poor Negroes, much less poor Whites. Poor Whites are about the worse thing that you can work for, because they've been poor all their lives and they want to make sure that you don't get anything. Since you are Black, they feel like you don't have any right to anything, so I never—if anytime somebody would offer me a job I would find out—I was very particular about where the people lived, what their neighborhood was. And if I found out it was in a certain neighborhood, then I don't want it. Because they don't have much more than I have and so I don't want to work for anybody like that. Work for somebody that can pay you.

This statement is particularly interesting, not merely because it presents her conception of the right working environment, but primarily because it provides considerable insight into her perceptions of society and her place within it. Through her jobs, she had come into contact with very wealthy people. She pointed out that she had worked for the family of one of the partners in a world-wide banking house based on New York City, and for one branch of the first families of Boston; that she rarely held a job where there was only one household worker; and that in her catering work in large churches on Fifth and Park Avenues, she had met dignitaries from England and other parts of the world. In this way, she did gain concrete knowledge of who the rich and powerful people were and how they lived.

By contrast, she raised her children in a predominantly White neighborhood which she described as being mostly working and middle-class, with a few poor Whites. Later, when her children were in their teens, she and her husband bought a home in a lower middle income residential area in the Bronx. Her residential pattern, her statements about classes of people and the ways in which she chose to talk about her jobs, indicate that while she describes herself as poor, her status identifications, values, and aspirations are middle class.

As the above statement shows, her concept of class is interwoven with her concept of race. Although she does not talk as much about social distinctions among blacks as she does those among Whites, it is clear that she is aware of wide variations within the Black community. Throughout the interview, she referred to the general living conditions Black people confronted in the '30s and '40s using it as a kind of backdrop to her life story. For example, at the beginning of the interview, when asked to describe how she began in housework and how she got her first job, she replied:

> When I came out of school, the Black man naturally had very few chances of doing certain things and even persons that I know myself who had finished four years of college were doing the same type of work because they couldn't get any other kind of work in New York.

Unlike Mrs. Prieleau, whose strong sense of social and racial identity is presented in very personal terms, Mrs. Tucker's is impersonally presented. Above, for example, race appears as a justification for doing domestic work. In general, she used the interaction between race and class to make very sharp and clear distinctions between groups of people in the society. The resulting categories and her notions of the behavioral traits associated with them, became a means of socially locating the people whom she encountered in her life. Interestingly, while she locates everyone else socially, she never really locates herself other than as a member of her family of procreation. Jewell Prieleau identified macro-social groupings which she labeled "we" and "they," yet Mrs. Tucker talks only about "they."

A partial explanation for this difference between the two women may lie in the different ways in which each woman experienced her work. While racial discrimination was a very personal experience for both, limiting their opportunities for employment outside of housework, their work experiences, and more importantly, the perceived impact of their work upon other aspects of their lives differed greatly. Mrs. Tucker perceived that she was not "handicapped by going out to work at all." In a word, she did not feel that her family life suffered from the demands of work. Yet, she did feel stigmatized by her work, a feeling most clearly communicated in the ambivalently defensive quality of her statements about the work itself. As pointed out above, she sought to minimize this feeling by working in the "right environment," and maintaining a sense of self that was not limited by the confines of her jobs. Her defensiveness about doing household work appears to arise from the same source, the conflict between her middle class identification and her real occupational status. Mrs. Prieleau, on the other hand, did feel that she was "handicapped" by her work. She describes her work as a major obstacle to a more pleasant and stable family life. The wounds of discrimination appear to be more painfully felt by Mrs. Prieleau who creates a direct linkage between being a poor Black woman alone and her daughter's nervous breakdown or her grandchild's death from lead poisoning. Her sense of self is devoid of the internal status discrepancies which Mrs. Tucker exhibits. Perhaps because discrimination and poverty were more painfully and bitterly experienced in Mrs. Prieleau's life, they were more difficult to objectify, even in conversation.

Lena Hudson, Jewell Prieleau, and Opallou Tucker tell very different stories of struggle and survival and of work and family. Their jobs, family lives, and world views differ considerably yet there are some important commonalities. Among these are a desire for education and upward mobility for their children or grandchildren; a concern for their children's well-being in a hostile and unsafe city; a definite sense of social location and of the social distance between their employers and themselves; and an acute consciousness of the opportunities and limitations of their individual work situations. The differences between their lives expand our perspective on a number of other questions which this study seeks to answer. The stories suggest, for example, that the particular arrangements of a woman's family life may have influenced the type of jobs she took or the ways in which she used her work situation to accomplish some personal or family goals. They also present three different adaptations to the class and racial inequities which separate the women from their employers. Mrs. Hudson is accepting of the disparities, Mrs. Prieleau resents them, and Mrs. Tucker, more than either of the others, identifies with the employing class. The two data chapters which follow examine these themes in greater depth and across the entire sample. The contradictions and similarities surrounding a given theme are explored in all of the self-histories which constitute the data for this study.

NOTES

1.   Jane Hallowell Coles and Robert Coles, *Women of Crisis* (New York: Delacorte Press, 1978), p. 232.

2.   A very insightful discussion of the social psychological consequences of oppression for both the oppressor and the oppressed is found in Albert Memmi, *The Colonizer and the Colonized* (Boston: Beacon Press, 1965). Memmi has also examined these issues with direct reference to servants in Albert Memmi, *Dominated Man* (Boston: Beacon Pres, 1968).

3.   For a fuller discussion of "surrogate mothers," see Chapter Five.

CHAPTER FOUR

WORK AND PERSONAL DIGNITY

This chapter explores the ways in which the women's self-perceptions of their work convey their struggle to make a socially deprecated occupation personally meaningful and rewarding. Specifically, it examines their characterizations of the work, degrees of identification with it, and the impact of its social stigma on their perceptions of themselves and their employers. As is indicated in Chapter Five, these factors are integrally related to the women's childrearing strategies and to the interaction of work and family in their lives.

Most of the women who participated in this study were keenly aware of the low social status of the occupation, yet they rarely presented themselves as defeated by it. Instead, they portrayed themselves as having been actively engaged in a struggle to assert their individual worth within the occupation. Their stories about work depict them as attempting to gain mastery over a situation in which they were defined as subjects. In other words, they sought to gain autonomy and control over their tasks and dignity in the mistress-servant relationship.

Contrary to popular imagery, the overriding attitude expressed toward the occupation was not disdain or loathing, but ambivalence.

I don't think domestic work is demeaning work. It's what people make it—like you have to use the back elevators, and can't eat the same food. . . . It's not demeaning work to do. (Zenobia King)

So many people have gotten their education by it, and it isn't any disgrace. . . . I wasn't embarrassed that I'd done that work because I knew I was prepared for something else. I did it because it was something I could do to help my husband out. . . . I think I should be proud and want to work. Domestic work is nothing to be ashamed of, but it's an art, just like anything else. You just have to learn how to do it. (Corrine Raines)

I mean people don't advertise it, but at the same time if they have a good job, they are not particularly ashamed of it, it's nothing to be ashamed of. You see, I think a lot of times we go into this business of talking about a menial task and that's what puts a lot of us on welfare. (Opallou Tucker)

First you got to make your job good yourself. You work at it everyday. . . . The only thing about it is that we have to learn how to live with your job. Your job is your livin' and you learn how to do it good. Nothin' is perfect. (Queenie Watkins)

In these comments, the women talk about not being embarrassed, disgraced, demeaned, or made to feel ashamed of being household workers. At the same time, these terms of derogation are counterposed against positively stated characteristics of the work, such as its being an art, a source of pride and satisfaction; and exhortations to the workers to work hard and *make* their jobs rewarding. While all four women seek to provide a strong defense of the worthiness of their life's work, it should be noted that their statements are defensive ones, reading more like disclaimers than acclamations. Corrine Raines says she wasn't embarrassed because she knew she could do something else, while Opallou Tucker argues that it's a lot better than being on welfare. These are essentially negative arguments in support of domestic service and reflect a feeling on the part of the women that they must defend or justify the dignity and merit of their work to others. This defensive posture is largely a response to the stigma attached to domestic service and to domestic service workers. Erving Goffman explains these reactions as follows:

The standards . . . incorporated from the wider society equip him (the stigmatized individual) to be intimately alive to what others see as his failing, to agree that he does indeed fall short of what he really ought to be. Shame becomes a central possibility.[1]

However, these statements also have a positive side; one which conveys the worker's determination to make her occupational role personally meaningful and socially acceptable. When Zenobia King states that domestic service is "what people make it," she acknowledges that the work is not inherently odious or menial but that the negative associations are socially created and can therefore be changed. Queenie Watkins suggests that the worker herself has more power and influence over the job than even she perhaps realizes.

Underlying these ambivalent feelings toward household work are three structural conditions. The highly personalized employer-employee relationship and the resulting lack of standardization of the work; attitudes in the Black community toward domestic work; and the individual worker's degree of affiliation with the work.

In Chapter One, the personalized nature of the employer-employee relationship was identified as a major contributing factor to the low status of the occupation. Clearly, the individual worker in this setting has fewer protections and is subject to greater exploitation. On the other hand, the intimacy which can develop between an employer and employee, along with the lack of job standardization may increase the employee's leverage in the relationship and give her some latitude within which to negotiate a work plan that meets her own interests and desires.

A second important factor that influenced the ways in which participants in this study viewed their work is the perspective within the Black community and, more specifically, among friends and family toward domestic service. Though the data in this study do not address this issue directly, we may derive an answer from a variety of factors. The high concentration of Black women in the occupation has had a major influence on community attitudes. As indicated in Table 2, between 1890 and 1960 more Black women in the labor force were classified as domestics or private household workers than in any other single occupational category. It is reasonable to assume that these women provided a network of support and reinforcement for one another. Jewell Prieleau confirmed this in her description of the social clubs in which she participated:

> In the late '40s and the '50s domestic girls used to get together
> and have clubs, social clubs. We would put money away all
> year and then at the end of the year we would have a big
> dance someplace. At the time the girls work in bars and girls

TABLE 2

OCCUPATIONAL DISTRIBUTION OF NEGRO WOMEN BY YEAR (PERCENT)

Occupation	1890	1930	1960	1970
Domestic	52	63	60	45
Private household			37	18
Other service			23	27
Agriculture	44	27	4[a]	_[b]
Manufacturing	3	5	16[c]	19[c]
Professional	1	3	8	12
Clerical	_[b]	_[b]	10	20

[a]Includes farmers and farm managers, farm laborers, and foremen.
[b]Less than one percent.
[c]Includes craftsmen and foremen, operatives, and non-farm laborers.

Source: U.S. Department of Labor, Women's Bureau, *Negro Women Worker*, by J. C. Brown, Bulletin No. 165 (Washington, D.C.: Government Printing Office, 1938); Donald J. Trieman and Kermit Terrell, "Women, Work, and Wages—Trends in the Female Occupation Structure" in Kenneth C. Lane and Seymour Spilerman, eds., *Social Indicator Models* (New York: Russell Sage Foundation, 1975), p. 160.

The importance of finding a "good" employer could not be overestimated and the women who participated in this study tended to equate an employer's social status with the quality of the job. In general, high status employers were thought to be better employers. Many discussions of household work have assumed that workers acquired status in direct relationship to the power, prestige, and wealth of their employers. Katzman, however, argues that "there is nothing to support the assumption that within their own community Black domestics attained high prestige by virtue of the social standing of their employing family."[4] The data collected in this study suggest that while status transfer was a concern for some workers, their employer's social position was important for other reasons. In some cases, personal recognition and interaction with people of wealth and power increased a worker's feelings of self-worth and her sense of the value of her own work. More important, however, was the belief that high status employers were better able to pay high salaries and provide liberal fringe benefits such as social security, sick leave, vacation pay, and holiday bonuses. Workers felt that they were more likely to have a good working relationship in high status families because these people were likely to have had prior experience managing household help and would therefore be both fair and generous. Thus, the attraction to wealthy and powerful employers was a logical and reasonable aspiration and these jobs came to represent the top rung of the occupational ladder.

By the same token, the personalized quality of the work relationship did have negative repercussions for some workers. An example was revealed in a statement made by Mattie Washington. In response to a question about the number of years she had worked for a particular family, she replied: "It's been thirty-three years. I say I gave them all my youth life." The idea that a household employee could give any portion of her life to an employer's family is both powerful and poignant. It implies a relationship that reaches out beyond the bounds of any job description and into the very depths of the employee's personal goals, aspirations, and daily life. As such, it suggests the possibility of commitment to the work relationship at the expense of or in substitution for personal commitments outside of work. Her statement, therefore, is also a mournful one, made even more somber by the recognition that the relationship is one of inequality and that Mattie Washington did not give her youth freely, but "gave" to those with the social and economic resources necessary to purchase it. In giving herself to them, she also gave up an opportunity to raise her own

daughter, to marry and to have a life separate from her life at work. Thus, she became even more dependent on her employer's beneficence and on a warm and affectionate relationship with their child.

Among the women who participated in this study, Mattie Washington's story is unusual. No one else described herself as giving or giving up so much for her job. Nevertheless, Mrs. Washington's story is important because it accentuates and thereby reveals in its most extreme form a fundamental tension of the employer-employee relationship in domestic service. On the one hand, most employers needed as much of a worker's time as they could get. From their perspective, the full-time, live-in servant who was on call twenty-four hours of the day would have been ideal. The worker, on the other hand, needed to protect as much of her personal life and time as she could. Therefore, the relationship could easily develop a dynamic in which the employee was either pulled toward relinquishing some control over her personal time or learned to set limits on her job. According to Katzman:

> Beneath the amenities of the mistress-servant relationship was a struggle between the two. Employers exercised as much power as they could, while domestics attempted to control their own labor and lives and retain their personal dignity.[5]

The women who participated in this study emphasized the idea that setting limits was an important strategy for survival in the occupation.

Stories of Resistance

One of the most interesting patterns through which the process of negotiating the employer-employee relationship is revealed is in what I have labeled "stories of resistance." Almost without exception, the women in this study related incidents in which they used confrontation, chicanery, or cajolery to establish limits for themselves within a particular household. In other words, they sought to define very carefully what they would and would not give to their employers in the way of time, commitment, and personal involvement. The basic message which these stories communicate is, that at least on some matters, the employee did not permit the employer to push her around. Oneida Harris, in the story below, suggests that this kind of resistance was

critical to the worker's maintenance of self-respect and that learning it early in her career increased her ability to survive.

> At the time I was very young and I didn't know how to cope. It was my first job. Maybe the children would come in from school and the floor might be a little damp. . . . She'd say, "Oh, you didn't scrub the kitchen floor today." I said, "Sure, I scrubbed it." She said, "Look at all that dirt." I said, "Well, one of the children came in." She said, "That dirt was there when I left—you just a liar and that's all!" That was unpleasant. . . . The thing I had to learn was not to let it get to me, and to call her a liar back. My aunt says, "Listen, you've got to learn when you work for people, to treat them as they treat you. If they're nice and sweet you can be that too. But if they use bad words to you, you gotta use 'em back. . . ." That's what I had to learn to do. I had to learn not to cry 'bout it, but to find some kind of way to get back at her. And that way I survived.

Fighting back as a key to survival in the occupation was a recurrent theme in the women's life histories. While Oneida Harris provides some insight into her personal struggle to acquire these skills, Bea Rivers' story focuses upon the utilization of these skills to protect her rights, as she saw them.

> One weekend her (the employer's) boyfriend was having a party and so she said, "You'll have to cook the turkey because it's Paul's birthday." I said all right. But this weekend, I think my sister was sick and I decided I would not go back to work. So I called her (the employer) and she got real nasty. Well, I hung up and then she called me back. She apologized and said she was sorry she had just got upset. I told her it was all right. When I came back, she said to me, "Well, one thing about you, Bea, nobody could every say anybody took advantage of you." I said, "Well maybe they can't say it, but you certainly have tried. The only difference is you didn't succeed because this job here is *your job*. This job is not the type of job that I have to live with the rest of my life. I lived before I ever came here and I could leave here and go back to the city and find

another job. Don't ever feel that this is the only job. When I came here I didn't sign any contract. I work here and I do enjoy it, but if there comes a time when things can be so unpleasant that I no longer enjoy it. . . . Now when you call me when I'm on leave and I'm home for a weekend and do a thing like that and I'm staying home on account of my sister's sick, it makes me feel very bad towards you. It means that you only live for yourself."

The determination to fight back was tied to the worker's perceptions of herself in relationship to her job. Beatrice Rivers' comments to her employer suggest that she had established clear boundaries between her own life and her work. Her statement may be read as an assertion of her independence; independence which is epitomized in the phrase "this job here is your job." With these words she indicates her refusal to "own" the job, to make it hers and to identify fully with it. It follows, therefore, that she would be unwilling to suppress her needs in favor of those of her employer, in spite of the fact that she needed and enjoyed the job. Instead, she characterizes her employer's behavior as an infringement on her rights, an attempt to "take advantage" of her. This kind of detachment from the job provides a buffer against the employer's insensitivity to her personal needs. In essence, the employer rejected Bea Rivers' sense of her own humanity by refusing to give her the personal considerations Bea felt she so often gave to the employer. A degree of detachment from the job, even if expressed only in a pique of anger, was an important defense in managing the relationship.

Direct confrontation with an employer and threats to quit were two of several strategies the women developed to resist what they considered to be unreasonable treatment. However, their stories indicate that these techniques were not employed capriciously. Most of the women needed their jobs, otherwise they would not have taken them. Like Bea Rivers, however, they describe themselves as making it clear to their employers that they were not in such desperate need that they would jeopardize their sense of self-worth. Thus, many used more indirect strategies to relate to their employers.

I went to the employment agency and I'd have to take what she'd give me and try 'cause I needed to work and I needed to make ends meet. But, I always used to interview them (employers). In fact, I used to make a lot of them very mad because I'd ask them all those questions about why their girl had quit and what did her duties entail, and what kind of work did they want done and what I would and what I wouldn't do. And I made some of them very angry. (Helen Satterwhite)

Through these "interviews," Mrs. Satterwhite not only gathers useful information about the work itself but gains insight into the employer. Her approach is an attempt to establish a degree of respect and dignity for herself at the outset of the relationship.

Chicanery was another strategy which the women used to establish their position with an employer.

This other family was very prejudiced. She's always show me things in the paper about colored people. One day she asked me, "Where did all the bad colored people come from?" I said, "I really wouldn't know, any more than you would know where all the bad White people come from." To put a stop to this, one day I showed her a clipping in the paper where some White [men] had robbed a bank. I said, "Oh, look at this, isn't this terrible. They robbed a bank. And they're White too!" After that she never showed me those clippings anymore. (Zenobia King)

Helen Satterwhite related the following incident:

She (the employer) told me what she wanted done and then she said, "My girl always scrubs the floor." Well, I noticed down in the basement that she had a mop and she had taken the mop and hid it. So I cleaned the whole house and everything, but I didn't mop the floors. And when I got ready to go, I took the bucket, the brush, and the kneepad and set them in the corner. When she came in she was very pleased. She said the house looks beautiful, you've done a lovely job. She went into the kitchen and she looked and she said, "But you didn't scrub the floor." She had a daughter who was ten years old, and I know I'm not her girl, I'm just the lady who came in to do the days work. So I said, "Well, you said your girl cleans the floor and I'm not your girl . . . and I don't

scrub floors on my hands and knees. "Well," she said,
"tomorrow I'll go out and buy a mop." So I got my coat on
and got ready to go and I said, "Why don't you just let me go
down in the basement and bring the mop up?"

These stories are reminiscent of the B'rer Rabbit tales of African
American folklore. It has the same message of the allegedly weaker
character; the rabbit in the folktales and the maid in the story, cleverly
outwitting and gaining a victory over a stronger or more powerful
adversary.[6] It is interesting, but not surprising, that this type of story
should appear among the life histories of a group of household workers.
As an oppressed group whose working conditions carried many
remnants of slavery, the stories convey their struggle to assert their
human rights in the fact of seemingly overwhelming obstacles. The
strategies which are used in the stories above; establishing oneself as
independent, using chicanery, and fighting back, represent the worker's
attempt to achieve some kinds of parity within the confines of a
relationship of domination.

Ultimately, of course, the workers could walk out of the
relationship and many women did. Quitting was a major item in the
women's histories and, in some ways, the ultimate form of resistance.
Katzman has suggested that "quitting a position [was] the only way to
improve conditions that were available to a servant."[7] However, for
most of the participants in this study, it was the ultimate weapon and
was always preceded by other defensive strategies. Without exception,
these women characterized themselves as leaving jobs when *they* tired
of them. Only one woman admitted ever having been fired from a job,
and she was quick to insist that this was the *only* such instance in her
entire working career. Queenie Watkins told the following story about
quitting:

I worked there with them until she made me angry one
morning. I had a bad toe and the doctor had told me to stay
off my feet. Her mother wanted to have a seder dinner there.
I had entertained Christmas and Thanksgiving and I said, "This
is too much. You know the doctor told me to stay off o' my
foot, and I just can't take care of fifteen people." She said,
"Well I'll just tell my mother you can't." That Thursday
morning, I went to take her breakfast on the tray—she had a

friend that spent the night with her. When I went in I heard this woman say to her, "You do what I do, tell her if she can't do it you'll hire somebody else who will. Nothing wrong with her. What's a drain in her toe?" I got so angry. I heard what she said. When I set the tray down she (the employer) said, "Queenie, I just got through talking to my mother and she wants the seder here. If you can't serve it, I'll hire somebody who will." I said, "Mrs. Jonas, this is your job, you do what you want to with it." And I never said another word. I just walked right out and started to pack my clothes.

Queenie Watkins' irate pronouncement to her employer that "this is your job" is reminiscent of Mrs. Rivers' statement above. Again, the work situation was described as pleasant, enjoyable and rewarding, carrying with it some degree of responsibility and autonomy and affording recognition for work that was well done. Also, both women considered their pay to be adequate. Nevertheless, at the point of confrontation, they indicated considerable readiness to dissociate themselves from the job, symbolically throwing it back in the employer's face. All of this suggests that the employer-employee relationship represents a fragile peace. The basic opposition of interests of the two parties and the self-protective behavior of employees which is its result, are two possible reasons for the instability inherent in the relationship. Albert Memmi, however, offers a related but slightly different explanation:

Domestic alienation is one in which the desire to identify with the master is at the same time the strongest and the most thwarted. . . . Their lives are . . . so interwoven, by the very practice of the daily job, that they are in a way part of each other, so that it would be impossible for the servant to withdraw himself. . . . However, this forced identification is condemned, by definition, to remain an illusion, There will never be a complete identification for there is a kind of denaturation of all the servant's acts, no matter how hard he applies himself. . . . This thwarted hope, this feeling of coming as close as possible and yet remaining infinitely far away, creates a state of unbearable tension.[8]

It is the tension of the master-servant relationship that explodes in Mrs. Rivers' and Mrs. Watkins' statements. They react angrily to their employers, as if betrayed. The action which is portrayed as betrayal in these stories is the employer's denial of the employee's humanity. In both cases, the employers are depicted as crude and unfeeling people, riding roughshod over the worker's human concerns and feelings; the very things which, in the worker's opinion, make her like everyone else. To ignore those things is to treat her like a machine and to negate the last, yet most important, shred of identity between them. The statement "this is your job" can thus be understood on two levels: it is the worker's reminder of the boundaries between herself and her job, and it is her angry rejection of the employing family because those boundaries cannot be penetrated. At either level, it is a statement of her alienation. On the first level it operates as a defensive, self-protective strategy; on the second, it is an act of aggression.

It is apparent from examining the data that the stories of resistance crystallize around the worker's feeling that their rights were always subject to violation, and that they must be prepared to defend and assert their humanity to make the work situation tolerable or to terminate it with a sense of self-respect. As Bea Rivers points out, it is not that her employer did not try to take advantage of her, she did not succeed because of Mrs. Rivers' resistance.

The stories of resistance are assertions of self-respect. They seek to dispel the notion that anyone who did domestic work was so desperate and downtrodden, she would do whatever was required to keep a job. While this need derives from the defensive position of an oppressed group, it indicates that the women perceived a certain degree of autonomy and flexibility within their overall situation. The data clearly indicate that they recognized a variety of types of jobs and employers within the field of private household work, and that they felt they had some choice in the matter of who they worked for and some control over the work relationship. Nevertheless, while some women's histories emphasized the freedom and autonomy they found within the field, others focused upon their feelings of being confined to a low-status occupational category.

Careers

Pearl Runner described her feelings about doing private household work this way:

> I didn't really want to do it, but I didn't have no choice because I didn't have the education to do what I like to do. My husband and I were struggling and I had to help him some way. So I made myself satisfied, let's put it that way, I made myself satisfied.

Opallou Tucker provides a different reason for doing domestic work but suggests that she too had limited options.

> When I came out of school the Black man naturally had very few chances of doing certain things and even persons that I know myself who had finished four years of college were doing the same type of work because they couldn't get any other kind in New York. . . . When they advertised for household help it was either for White or light colored. You had to be a certain size because the people only bought uniforms for certain size women. . . . Just before I got married I started to doing housework, and it's no different from doing your own housework, if you work for somebody who's decent, which I've always done. I'd never work for anyone who was impossible.

Poverty, lack of education, and discrimination are the forces which are identified as impinging upon both women's ability to freely determine their occupation. At the same time, there is considerable difference in the tone of these two statements. Mrs. Runner conveys a sense of resignation to a fate over which she felt she had little control. Unlike Mrs. Tucker, who emphasizes her ability to change the work to make it suit her needs, Mrs. Runner focuses upon adapting to the work as she found it. The contrast in these two women's feelings about themselves in relationship to the work reflects a dichotomy which is apparent throughout the data. It is the difference between those women, like Mrs. Tucker, who made careers of domestic service and those, like Mrs. Runner, who did not.

Only five of the women who participated in this study can be considered part of the non-career group. These five described themselves as having done domestic work off and on for about ten years, in contrast to the career women who had worked in service for thirty or more years. In addition, their period of work as a household employee was generally early in their lives and they were not always able to tell the interviewer precisely when and how long they had worked on various jobs. A major reason, in addition to that of forgetting, was that they had held other jobs during their working lives and these were more salient and important to them. One woman, Georgia Sims, when asked to talk about her experience in domestic work, replied as follows:

> I don't see nothing experienced about domestic work. . . . I mean you went to work, you scrubbed, you was doing floors. You come home, that's all; day by day, same thing every day just different apartments that's all. . . . Most of the best I've had is from Schraft's (a food service business where she had worked in the kitchen).

A second woman, upon being asked to discuss her most pleasant experiences in household work, said:

> None. Wasn't pleasant at all. . . . I didn't care too much for domestic work. . . . I liked the job [with a railroad line] in every respect, from the time I got it 'til the time I left it. I love people and I was always among people. See, being a clerk in the [railroad] you have to know how to handle people. And I got along with people really well.

Like Mrs. Runner, her attitude towards household work was almost totally negative and both women described themselves as doing it out of necessity. Their feelings that it was unpleasant work were expressed openly and without ambivalence. Notably, their dislike of the occupation seemed to be focused more on the lack of choice, its monotony, drudgery, and low social status than upon any particularly unpleasant employers. Since almost of all of the women, career and non-career, had had pleasant and unpleasant employers, this did not seem to be a major factor differentiating them. In general, the non-career women did not portray themselves as actively engaged in creating opportunities for self-satisfaction and reward within the occupation, but minimized their years in household work, giving the impression that they had left it as soon as an opportunity arose.

While these factors mark the broad distinctions between the career and non-career women, there were, of course, similarities in the ways in which both sets of women related to their work. Many of the career women worked in different types of jobs for some period of time and several of them expressed the desire to have had a different occupation. Non-career women, for the period of time they were in domestic service, seemed to have become somewhat engaged in the struggle to gain mastery over the work and to assert their independence and self-respect.

Nevertheless, the tone and structure of the self-histories reflect the overall difference between the two groups. The non-career women are very distant from their experiences as household workers. Like Georgia Sims, they saw little to elaborate about and had few stories to relate. For the most part, stories of resistance are absent from their autobiographies. The career women, on the other hand, through their descriptions of their jobs and employers, vividly recreated their experiences in household work with all of the conflicts and contradictions. Their self-histories have a narrative texture and pace which capture a range of complex emotions: anger, tenderness, love, hatred, disgust and triumph. The reader comes away from these histories with a fuller understanding of the rewards and detractions of the occupation.

Most importantly, career women's lives exhibit just that—a *career* in domestic service. Everett C. Hughes has stated that "the career includes not only the processes and sequences of learning the techniques of the occupation, but also the progressive perception of the whole system of possible places in it and the accompanying changes in conceptions of the work and one's self in relation to it."[9] The life stories of the career women focus primarily upon their perceptions of the "whole system of possible places within" the occupation of private household work. Their stories of resistance and the sense they create of being involved in an ongoing struggle to gain mastery over the work provide adequate testimony to this contention. In addition, there is a distinct pattern that characterizes their career, one which indicates an increasing knowledge of the types of jobs, employers, and income associated with the work, marked by a point at which most settled into one particular job that offered increased security, comfort, and satisfaction.

The self-histories provide considerable insight into the women's changing perceptions of the occupation and their relationship to it. The stories they related about their early experiences in the field as well as their occupational mobility reveal some interesting patterns and provide greater insight into their struggle for self-respect. Jewell Prieleau told the following story about her first job in service in the North:

> When I first came [North], I was sent here by a minister. He was like an agency down there and these people would send the money to him and he'd put you on a ship and send you here—second class, of course. That was [in about 1936]. So the people would meet you right to the boat, take you off the boat. And they'd put you right on the floor to scrub or to mop. When he send you to that family it was like you was bought. . . . And you had to work until you pay the money back no matter what happened.

Her description of the event indicates that she was keenly aware of her status as an indentured servant and of the similarity between her circumstances and those of ancestors being brought to this country centuries before. She describes herself as being moved around like a piece of cargo, "put on" and "taken off" the ship, "put on the floor to scrub or to mop." Her feelings about the experience are conveyed in the same depersonalized language. In fact, she has virtually absented herself from the story. The "you" to whom she refers is not Jewell Prieleau as much as it is an abstraction, any young female migrant from the South who had become an indentured servant. Part of the distance between herself and the "you" to whom she refers is a result of time: the incident occurred almost forty years before she recounted it to the interviewer. However, it also reflects a detached perception of herself in relationship to the work. Unlike her descriptions of incidents which occurred more recently, she does not convey any feeling of attachment either to members of the family for whom she worked or to the work itself. Neither does she express the ambivalence which was characteristic of most of the "career" women's statements.

Another experience which typified many women's early years and shaped their later feelings about their work was in the "slave markets." During the 1930s, when most of the participants in this study were entering the field of household employment in the North, "slave markets" developed in several cities. The Bronx, New York, was particularly notorious as a place that offered degrading and exploitative conditions for household workers, but it was not the only place where these practices occurred.[10] Many of the women talked about these marketplaces for domestic service in other sections of New York as well as in Philadelphia. Two descriptions follow:

It wasn't easy to get jobs. You would go and stand on the corner and people would come out and pick you up. Everybody in North Philly (Philadelphia) was standing on corners to get work. And I was mostly the smallest one there and they would look all over me. One day one lady came by and she said, "Well, you look like you're the only one here so I'm gonna have to take you, but you certainly don't look like you can do the work. . . ." It was very hard housework. They wanted you to scrub floors and windows and all kinds of stuff. Those were the first jobs I had when I came up here. (Helen Satterwhite)

You would go to the Bronx and there was certain corners that you would sit on. So some people had a box they would sit on, some lean up against a store or wall. . . . And they would come and just pick out a nice clean girl they thought they could trust. And you worked, thirty-five cents an hour or a quarter, or when you finished they give you what they thought—which was good in times like that (circa 1937). (Jewell Prieleau)

It is not surprising that these street corner recruitment sites were labeled "slave markets" in some of the literature of that day. Like Mrs. Prieleau's story of being shipped to New York, they recall images of slavery which merely served to reinforce the low social status of the occupation. One of the most striking aspects of these descriptions, however, is that while the women present themselves as selling their labor on the street corners, they also had to convey the fact that their entire person was evaluated as part of the sale. They had to look trustworthy, reliable, strong, and clean in order to be selected for a day of heavy housework. It was not sufficient to appear on the corner, desperately in need of a day's work. They had to be willing to subject their very being to the scrutiny of women who were shopping for a person to clean their homes.

These descriptions of early experiences in household employment demonstrate a kind of objectification of the woman as worker. The women seem to see themselves being made synonymous with the work itself, becoming a mere instrument by which the tasks of housework were to be carried out. Oakley's description of the relationship of the housewife to her work may readily be extended to the housewife's employee, the household worker. She says:

> The housewife, in an important sense IS her job: separation between subjective and objective elements in the situation is therefore intrinsically more difficult. This is an important point which is crucial to the whole question of attitudes to, and satisfaction with, housework.[11]

A major aspect of the worker's struggle to attain mastery over the work was directed against this objectification. In their self-histories they describe themselves as seeking and finding satisfaction in job situations where they received human and personal recognition. It has already been pointed out that the confrontations which were related in many stories of resistance were reactions to the employer's failure to recognize the employee's personal needs and concerns, their humanity. According to Goffman:

> The stigmatized individual tends to hold the same beliefs about identity that we do; this is a pivotal fact. His deepest feelings about what he is may be his sense of being a "normal person," a human being just like anyone else, a person therefore who deserves a fair chance and a fair break.[12]

While not every woman in the study shared these early negative experiences of being shipped to New York or looking for work in the "slave markets," all of them had experiences which served to remind them of their subservient position. Within this context the struggle for respect and mastery over the occupation takes on greater meaning.

The data indicate a common career pattern among the women who made careers of domestic work. Helen Satterwhite described it thus:

> I started off going to the employment agency. And the lady would send me out on a job and some of them were real rugged and nasty. And I'd work that one day, but I would never go back. And then, once you got with one good person, you didn't need to worry about anything else.

These sentiments were echoed and elaborated upon by Lena Hudson:

> When you first started out, you had to start out in the Bronx, and then on, as I say, one job always got me another. I was working for a lady once and she said to me, I hope to see you get into a family of people that would be really able to pay you for what you was worth. So you see, one job just got me to another.

The critical element in the process referred to above is gaining entrance into a circle of people who were deemed more likely to treat the employee with decency and dignity. Lena Hudson contrasted the employers on her later jobs with those she encountered while working in the Bronx.

> Those (later) jobs paid more. Well, that was a better class of people. . . . What I meant, they were more able to pay and quite natural, some of the job (in the Bronx), would take advantage of you because they know you had to work. . . . Well you know there is a difference in classes of people, how they handle you for what they are. If you work for a nice class of people, they recommend you to another, somebody in that category.

In this statement, Mrs. Hudson presents two ideas of class that are reiterated by most of the women in this study: one, that class is based on wealth; and two, that wealth influences the way in which an employer will treat their household help. She is quite explicit in stating that the ways in which different classes of people "handle" others is an outgrowth of their own class situation, not a response to the other's social position. The significance of this distinction for household workers is in the importance placed on an employer's social class as a criteria for determining a desirable work situation. According to Opallou Tucker:

> You find the richer they (employers) are, the more lenient they are and the better they are. . . . The poorer class is the class that don't want to do anything. Don't ever anybody go to work with one that's poor. They're going to be digging and digging all along because that poor Madam has gotten to the place where she can sit down. . . . And, of course, she's going to work you to death.

Mrs. Tucker's comments on this issue introduce the notion of inter-class conflict and competition. Her analysis points up the potential for rivalry among those who had recently obtained sufficient income to hire a household worker and those doing the work. From her perspective, the nouveau riche, or newly arrived middle income employers whom she labels "poor," hired household workers as a status symbol, and overworked them because they were cheap and they wanted maximum output for a minimal investment. As a worker, being employed in such a household offered few satisfactions in the form of social status, pay, fringe benefits or job-related responsibilities.

In reciting the advice which a former employer gave her about his daughter-in-law, Rosa Waters highlights this rivalry and repeats a belief that was prevalent in most of the women's discussions of class:

> He (the employer) said, you have to watch her (the daughter-in-law). *She's a poor girl and never been used to nothin', so she may not know how to treat you.* . . . And right then, she was taking my money. (Italics mine.)

The implication of this statement is that a person who is not used to having money or any of its accoutrements, such as servants, could not be trusted to treat the worker with dignity. Mrs. Waters' experience was not unique. Many of the women described themselves as having been exploited or overworked by "poor" employers.

Ella Baker and Marvel Cooke suggested that there was a kind of rivalry between household workers and their "poor" mistresses. They argued that this rivalry provided a partial explanation for the tense and exploitative conditions that developed in the Bronx "slave market." "The crash of 1929 expanded the ranks of people who could hire domestic workers and the exploiters, sadly enough, [were] descendants of tradespeople and artisans who battle[d] against being exploited themselves."[13] In their opinion, the struggle was between two groups of oppressed people fighting over a pittance that represented their small share of a larger economic whole.

Class rivalries and conflicts were compounded by racial animosities, particularly in the relationship between the nouveau riche and the household worker. Opallou Tucker summarized it in this manner:

> Poor Whites are just about the worse thing you can work for. Because they've been poor all their lives, they want to make sure you don't get anything. Because, since you're Black, you don't have the right to anything.

The notion that rich Whites are more generous and paternalistic towards Blacks has its roots deep in the slave experience, when the rivalry for social acceptance and dignity between Blacks and Whites was first nurtured.[14] It is not surprising, therefore, that its meaning would have had particular significance for a more contemporary relationship between servants and masters.

Class and race notwithstanding, working for the wealthy employer offered the worker greater social status and a chance to interact with the social elite. According to Corrine Raines,

> My most pleasant experience, in the later years, is doing catering for parties and preparing and decorating beautiful dishes. Very well-dressed people, very cultured people, come in and give me compliments on what I've done. I get some money or something. That's been some of my pleasure.

Mrs. Tucker said the following about her jobs:

> You have the opportunity, if you worked in the right environment, of meeting and coming into contact with some of the world's biggest people, men and women. In my work, I've come in contact with people and I mean not only just see them once. They visit these different places, different friends of theirs at different times. They remember you, they ask for you,

they come and talk to you. They talk to you about things in
their countries and things that are here. And it shows you that
you are not just a piece of furniture there.

As both women indicate, working in the right environment was a
means to increased self-respect. However, the rewards of the situations
described above were not only in feeling that they had overcome their
objectification as workers through the personal recognition they
received, but also because the people from whom they received this
recognition were among the social elite. Mrs. Tucker indicates that this
recognition made her feel as if she mattered as a person and was not
merely an object holding an hors d'oeuvre tray.

The attraction toward wealthy, high-status employers, however,
could have presented serious problems for the employee as Mattie
Washington's story suggests. Memmi's discussion of domestic
alienation referred to above implies that feelings of frustration and
tension would mount as the gulf between employer and employee
widened. Yet, the self-histories on which this study is based reflect little
hatred and hostility toward employers and little self-blame or self-doubt
on the part of employees.[15] This is perhaps because most of the women
who participated in the study had worked in domestic service for many
years, virtually all of their working lives. Unlike the few non-career
women who had left the occupation feeling mostly disdain for it, the
career women probably came to feel like Jewell Prieleau, who said:

When I was younger, I thought things like that but as I got
older I began to feel well, maybe that's the way it is so there's
nothing you can do about it. Some people are blessed and have
money and they just don't do anything.

Nevertheless, while even the career women accepted their place in
the social order with some equanimity, they did not give up or stop
believing in the American ideology of social mobility. At least, not for
their children.

NOTES

1. Erving Goffman, *Stigma* (Englewood Cliffs, N.J.: Prentice-Hall, p. 7.

2. Katzman, p. 246.

3. James Blackwell, *The Black Community* (New York: Dodd, Mead, & Co., 1975), p. 73.

4. Katzman, p. 247.

5. Katzman, p. 176.

6. J. Mason Brewer, *American Negro Folklore* (Chicago: Quadrangle Books, 1968), pp. 3-4.

7. Katzman, p. 222.

8. Albert Memmi, *Dominated Man* (Boston: Beacon Press, 1968), pp. 174-175.

9. Everett C. Hughes, "The Study of Occupations," in *Sociology Today: Problems and Prospects*, eds. Robert K. Merton, L. Broom and L. S. Cottrell, Jr. (New York: Harper Torchbooks, 1965), p. 456.

10. For descriptions of these "slave markets" see Gerda Lerner, ed. *Black Women in White America* (New York: Pantheon Books, 1972), Chapter 4; and Ella Baker and Marvel Cooke, "The Bronx Slave Market," *The Crisis: A Record of the Darker Races*, 42 (November 1935):330.

11. Oakley, *Housework*, p. 53.

12. Goffman, p. 7.

13. Baker and Cooke, pp. 330 and 341.

14. See Eugene Genovese, *Roll, Jordan, Roll* (New York: Pantheon, 1974), pp. 7-25.

15. These findings provide an interesting contrast with several other studies of working class people, where feelings of self-doubt and self-blame appear more important. See Richard Sennett and Jonathan Cobb, *The Hidden Injuries of Class* (New York: Knopf, 1972); and Lillian Rubin, *Worlds of Pain* (New York: Basic Books, 1976).

CHAPTER FIVE

CHILDREARING GOALS AND STRATEGIES

The childrearing goals and strategies adopted by the women who participated in this study are particularly revealing of the relationship of work and family. As working mothers, they were concerned with providing safe and secure care for their children while they were away from home. As working class people, seeking to advance their children beyond their own occupational achievements, they confronted the problem of guiding them towards goals that were outside their own personal experience. These issues, as well as others, take on a particular form for women who were household workers primarily because of the nature of the work. It was pointed out earlier that household workers often become vital participants in the daily lives of two separate families: their employer's and their own. In fact, they have often been described as being "like one of the family," and yet the barriers between them and their employers are real and immutable ones. In addition, we have seen that working class Black women employed by middle and upper middle class White families observe and experience vast differences in their material quality of life in the two homes. With regard to childrearing, employers could provide luxuries and experiences for their children that were well beyond the financial means of the employee.

This chapter, therefore, examines the ways the women talked about their reactions and responses to the discrepancies in life chances between their children and those of their employers. To some extent, these discrepancies became the lens through which their goals for their children and their childrearing practices were viewed. At the same time, the contrast in objective conditions provides a background against which the women's perceptions of similarities between themselves and their employers are made more interesting.

The data in this chapter indicate that the relationship between the employee's family life and her work was shaped by four basic factors. First, there was the structure of the work. Whether she worked full-time or part-time and lived in, lived out, or did "days work" determined the extent to which she became involved in the employer's day to day life. It also determined the amount of time she had to share with her own family. Second were the tasks and duties she was assigned. With regard to her own childrearing goals and strategies, the intermingling of employer and employee lifestyles occurred most frequently among those women who took care of the employer's children. It is through their discussion of these activities that the similarities and differences between the two families are most sharply revealed. A third factor is the degree of employer-employee intimacy. An employee who took care of the employer's children was more likely to have an intimate relationship with her employing family, but not always. Though the employer-employee relationship in domestic service is a personalized one when compared with other work relationships, this does not presume intimacy—a reciprocal exchange of interests and concerns—between the two parties. Among the women who participated in this study, those who did not share much of their own life with their employers appeared to minimize the interaction of work and family. Finally, were the employee's goals for her children. Those women who felt that their employers could aid them in achieving the educational or other goals they had for their children were more likely to encourage an intermingling of these two parts of their lives. These four factors were the primary structural determinants of the relationship between work and family. However, they operate within the context of the woman's entire sense of herself, her life, and her personal philosophy. It is for this reason that in analyzing the data structural factors are discussed within the context of the women's self-presentations.

Domestic Work and Upward Mobility

Strangely enough, I never intended for my children to have to work for anybody in the capacity that I worked. Never. And I never allowed my children to do any babysitting or anything of the sort. I figured it's enough for the mother to do it and in this day and time you don't have to do that. . . . So they never knew anything about going to work or anything. They went to school. (Opallou Tucker)

Given the low social status of the occupation, the ambivalent and defensive feelings many of the women expressed about their work, and the eagerness with which women left the occupation when other opportunities became available, it is not at all surprising that most of the women in this study said that they did not want their children to work in domestic service. Their hopes were centered upon "better" jobs for their children: jobs with more status, income, security, and comfort. Pearl Runner recalled her goals for her children:

> My main goals was I didn't want them to follow in my footsteps as far as working. I always wanted them to please go to school and get a good job because it's important. That was really my main object.

Lena Hudson explained her own similar feelings this way:

> They had a better chance than I had, and they shouldn't look back at what I was doing. They had a better chance and a better education that I had, so look out for something better than I was doing. And they did. I haven't had a one that had to do any housework or anything like that. So I think that's good.

The notion of a better chance was a dominant one in the women's discussion of their goals for their children. They portray themselves as struggling to give their children the skills and training they did not have, and as praying that opportunities which had not been open to them would be open for their children. In their life histories, the women describe many of the obstacles they encountered in this quest. Nevertheless, there are dilemmas which, though not discussed explicitly, are implicit in their narratives and a natural outgrowth of their aspirations.

First of these is the task of guiding children toward a future over which they had little control and toward occupational objectives they had not experienced. Closely tied to this problem was the need to communicate the undesirability of household work and at the same time maintain one's personal dignity. While these two problems are not exceptional for working class parents in an upwardly mobile society, they were mediated for Black domestic workers through the attitudes toward household work held by members of the Black communities in which the women lived and raised their children.

Had domestic work not been the primary occupation of Black women and had racial and sexual barriers not been so clearly identifiable as the reason for their concentration in this field of employment, these problems might have been viewed more personally and the women's histories might have been more self-deprecating than, in fact, they were. This particular set of circumstances would suggest that the women at least had the option of directing their anger and frustration about their situation outwards upon the society rather than turning it inward upon themselves. Drake and Cayton confirm this argument in their analysis of domestic work, saying that "colored girls are often bitter in their comments about a society which condemns them to 'White folks' kitchen."[1] In addition, as discussed in Chapter Four, attitudes in the Black community towards domestic service work provided a buffer against some of the more negative attitudes which were prevalent in the wider society. Thus, the community could potentially become an important support in the childrearing process, reinforcing the idea that while domestic service was low status work, the people who did it were not necessarily low status people.

It becomes obvious then that the complexities of the mother's situation would generate a variety of conflicting feelings about domestic work on the part of the children. One of the histories touches briefly on this issue. Opallou Tucker recounted the following story:

> When they were going to school they all made excellent marks . . . and they didn't have anything else to do but whatever they thought they would like to do. Like you take the youngest one, now she's not a housekeeper and she doesn't claim to be one. She told her sister one day, "I wasn't born to be a housekeeper, I was born to have servants."

Although this story was told with laughter and amusement, it offers revealing insights into one of the potential outcomes of this dilemma. On the one hand, Mrs. Tucker protested that she was not ashamed of her work but didn't want her children to do it; yet her daughter, feeling no need to justify the occupation, expressed total disdain for it. In fact, she does not even appear to object to the existence of a master-servant relationship. Her concern is to make sure that she is not among the servants. Mrs. Tucker was clearly proud of her daughter's attitude.

The data in this study do not include the attitudes of the children of domestic servants toward their mother's occupation and there has been no systematic study of this issue. However, some biographies and community studies have provided insight into the range of feelings children express. Drake and Cayton, for example, cite one woman who described her daughter as being "bitter against what she calls the American social system. . . ."[2] DuBois talks about feeling an instinctive hatred toward the occupation.[3] I have had employers tell me that their domestics' children hated their children because the employer's kids got the best of their mother's time. I have also heard Black professionals speak with a mixture of pride, anger, and embarrassment about the fact that their mother worked "in the White folk's kitchen" so that they could get an education. Clearly these issues deserve further study.

In all three of the statements cited at the beginning of this chapter, education was identified as the primary means through which mobility could be achieved. As with many working class people, education was seen as a primary strategy for upward mobility; a means to better paying and more prestigious jobs. Most of the women who participated in this study had not completed high school. (The mean years of schooling completed for the group was 9.2 years.) They reasoned that their limited education in combination with racial discrimination had hindered their own chances for upward mobility. Zenobia King explained her own attitudes toward education in this way:

> In my home in Virginia education I don't think was stressed. The best you could do was be a school teacher. It wasn't something people impressed upon you you could get. I had an aunt and cousin who were trained nurses and the best they could do was nursing somebody at home or something. They couldn't get a job in a hospital. . . . I didn't pay education any mind really until I came to New York. I'd gotten to a certain stage in domestic work in the country and I didn't see the need for it. When I came I could see opportunities that I could have had if I had a degree. People said it's too bad I didn't have a diploma.

From Mrs. King's perspective and from that of some other women, education for a Black woman in the South before World War II did not seem to offer any tangible rewards. She communicates the idea that an education was not only unnecessary but could perhaps have been a source of even greater frustration and dissatisfaction. This idea was reemphasized by other women who talked about college educated women they knew who could find no work other than domestic work. In fact, both Queenie Watkins and Corrine Raines discussed their own experiences as trained teachers who could not find suitable jobs and thus took work in domestic service. Nevertheless, Corrine Raines maintained her belief in education as a means of upward mobility, a belief that was rooted in her family of orientation. She said:

> I am the twelfth child [and was] born on a farm. My father was—at that day you would call him a successful farmer. He was a man who was eager for his children to get an education. Some of the older ones had gotten out of school and was working and they were able to help the younger ones. That's how he was able to give his children as much education as he gave them, because the older ones helped out.

Given this mixed experience with education and social mobility, it might be expected that many of them would have expressed reservations about the value of an education for their children's mobility. However, this was not the case. Most of them, in reflecting on their goals for their children, expressed sentiments similar to Pearl Runner's:

> This is the reason why I told them to get an education. . . . If they want to go to college it was fine because the higher you go the better jobs you get. They understood that because I always taught that into them. Please try to get an education so you can get a good job 'cause it was hard for colored girls to get jobs period. They had to have an education.

Mrs. Runner's statement is important because it contains the rudiments of an explanation for why she and other of the women stressed education in the face of discriminatory practices that frequently discounted even their best efforts. Opallou Tucker elaborates on this theme and provides a somewhat more detailed explanation:

It's (domestic work) all right if you want to do it and if you can't do anything else, but it's not necessary now. If you prepare yourself for something, prepare yourself for something that's better, the doors are open now. I know years ago there was no such thing as a Black typist. I remember girls who were taking typing when I was going to school. They were never able to get a job at it. So it really [was] for their own personal use. My third child, and a niece, after they got up some size, started taking typing. And, things began to open up after she got grown up. But in my day and time you could have been the greatest typist in the world, but you would never have gotten a job. It's fine to prepare yourself so that when opportunity knocks you'll be able to catch up.

In these statements, Mrs. Runner and Mrs. Tucker convey a complex and subtle understanding of the interaction of racism and opportunity. They recognize the former as a real and tangible barrier but they do not give in to it. They describe themselves as having taught their children to be prepared. Education was seen as a means of equipping oneself for whatever breaks might occur in the nation's pattern of racial exclusion. Thus, the key to their aspirations for their children was the hope and belief that opportunities would eventually open up and permit their children to make full use of the skills and knowledge they encouraged them to attain.

Nevertheless, maintaining these hopes could not have been as easy and unproblematic as hindsight makes it seem. Many of the women who expressed this strong commitment to education at the time of the interview had seen their dreams fulfilled. Their children completed a number of years of schooling and entered jobs which would never have been open to them when they were young. These accomplishments were a source of pride and satisfaction which could only have strengthened their beliefs. Thus, as they recalled their goals and aspirations for their children, they tended to speak with a sense of self-affirmation about their choices; confidence that may not have been present years earlier. Again, Mrs. Runner:

I will tell you I feel really proud and I really feel that with all the struggling that I went through, I feel happy and proud that I was able to keep helping my children, that they listened and that they all went to high school. So when I look back, I really

feel proud, even though at times the work was very hard and
I came home very tired. But now, I feel proud about it. They
all got their education.

Perhaps reflective of their understanding of the complex interaction
of racism and opportunity, most of the women described limited and
general educational objectives for their children. Although a few women
said they had wanted their children to go to college and one sent her
son to a private high school with the help of scholarships, most women
saw high school graduation as the concrete, realizable objective which
they could help their children attain. Willa Murray's story brings out a
theme that was recurrent in several other histories:

My children did not go to college. I could not afford to send
them to college. And they told me, my younger one especially,
he said, "Mommy, I don't want to go to college at your
expense. When I go to college, I'll go on my own. I would not
think of you workin' all your days—sometimes you go sick
and I don't know how you gonna get back. You put us through
school and you gave us a beautiful life. We'll get to college on
our own."

Mrs. Murray seems to indicate that while she would have liked for her
children to go to college, she limited her goals and concentrated her
energies upon their completing high school.
In addition to limited educational objectives, most of the women
did not describe themselves as having had a specific career objective in
mind for their children. They encouraged the children to get an
education in order to get a better job. Precisely what those jobs would
be was left open to be resolved through the interaction of their son or
daughter's own luck, skill, perseverance, and the overall position of the
job market regarding Black entrants.
Closely related to the goals the women expressed about their
children's future position in society were their goals relative to their
child's development as a person. Concern that their children grow up to
be good, decent, law-abiding citizens was a dominant theme in these
discussions. In the case study of Lena Hudson it was pointed out that
she expressed these kinds of goals and they contrasted with what she
perceived as her employers' goals for their children. Most of the women

in the study described their employers as having very specific career goals for their children, usually goals that would have had the children following in their parents' professional footsteps. In characterizing the differences between their goals and those of their employers, the women stressed the differences in economic resources. Johnnie Boatwright was quite explicit on this point:

> There was a lot of things they (employers) did that I wanted to do for mine, but I just couldn't afford it. . . . Like sending them to school. Then they could hire somebody; child slow, they could hire a tutor for the child. I wish I could have been able to do what they done. And then too, they sent them to camps, nice camps, not any camp but one they'd pick out. . . . So that's what I wished I coulda had did for him (her son). . . . See, whether it was right or wrong, mines I couldn't do it because I didn't have the money to do it. I wasn't able to do it. So that's the way it was. I did what I could and that was better than nothing.

In light of these discrepancies in resources, personal development was an important and realizable goal and emphasizing it may have been an adaptive response to the barriers which limited access to more specific career goals. Character development was an area over which the mothers had greater influence and potential control. It was also an area in which they probably received considerable community support since values in the Black community, as pointed out above, attribute status to success along personal and family dimensions in addition to occupation, education, and income.

While Mrs. Boatwright conveys a sense of resignation and defeat in discussing her inability to do for her son what the employers did for theirs, Pearl Runner is more optimistic and positive about what she was able to do for her children. She said:

> Their money may be a little more, but I felt my goals was just as important as long as they (the children) got their education. They (the employers) had the money to do lots more than I did, but I felt that if I kept working my goals was just as important. I felt my children were just as important.

Feelings like those expressed by both Mrs. Runner and Mrs. Boatwright are reflected throughout the data in the women's comparisons of their aspirations and expectations for their children's future with those of their employers. However, it also seems apparent that their intimate participation in families in which the husbands were doctors, lawyers, stockbrokers, college professors, and businessmen, and the wives were social workers college professors, writers, and housewives provided considerable support for their more limited educational objectives. While not everyone had the specific experience of Lena Hudson, whose employer gave her daughter an allowance which permitted her to stay in high school, the model of the employer's life, with regard to the kinds of things they were able to give their children, was a forceful one and is repeatedly reflected in the women's discussions of their childrearing goals.

The women who stressed education for their children and saw their children attain this education were frequently those women who were closely tied to one or two employing families for a long period of time. For the most part they were the women who were identified in Chapter Four as career women. However, this in itself was not critical because some women felt they had gotten very little support from their employers along these lines. Several women, as indicated above, pointed to a strong emphasis upon education in their families of orientation. Additionally, education as a means of upward mobility is a fundamental element in American social ideology. It appears, therefore, that the importance of the employer-employee relationship was in the support and reinforcement these middle class families' goals, aspirations, and style of life provided the women. The amount of support varied, of course, with the particular relationship that the employee had with her employer's family, and the degree of the employer's interest in and commitment to the employee's personal life. On the spectrum presented by the women in this study, Mrs. Hudson's relationship with the Wallis family would be at one end and the relationship between Georgia Sims and the family for whom she worked longer, at the other. The following segment of the interview with Mrs. Sims is a good example of a minimally interactive employer-employee relationship:

INTERVIEWER: What were your goals for your children?

MRS. SIMS: Well, to be decent, law-abiding men. That's all.

INTERVIEWER: Do you think there were any similarities between your goals for your children and the goals your employers, the Peters, had for their children?

MRS. SIMS: Oh, sure! Oh, yes, because I mean you must remember, they had the money; now I didn't have it. Oh, definitely, there was different goals between us.
(Note: Mrs. Sims obviously understands the question to be about *differences* rather than similarities, so the question was asked again.)

INTERVIEWER: Do you think there were any things that were alike in terms of your goals for your children and the goals for their children?

MRS. SIMS: No. Nothing.

INTERVIEWER: Nothing at all?

MRS. SIMS: No.

INTERVIEWER: What kinds of goals did they have for their children?

MRS. SIMS: Oh, I mean education, going on to be, you know, upstanding citizens, and they had the jobs—My children couldn't get up, I mean when they become twenty, twenty-one, they couldn't get up and say, well, I'm going on Fifth Avenue and I'm gonna get an office job. I'm gonna get this kind of job. No. The best thing they could do is go and be a porter in the subway.

In Chapter Four, Mrs. Sims was characterized as being very detached from the occupation. She was not a career household worker. In fact, she described herself as having had very limited contact with her employers; arriving when they were all on their way to work and school and often departing before they returned home. She said that she had no specific child care duties. Thus, her description of her employer's goals for their children is probably more of a projection on her part than it is based on discussion or direct participation in the employer's life.

Perhaps not coincidentally, Mrs. Sims was one of the women who was most negative about her children's life chances. She does not communicate the hope or the belief that things would change or that she could change them. Instead, she conveys a sense of resignation and bitterness about an oppressive fate. Unlike some of the women discussed earlier, she does not present herself as having focused her childrearing goals and strategies upon preparing her children for a better chance. While she may have wished that they would have had a better chance and had now lived to see the improvement, her description of herself when she was raising them does not present a view of poverty and discrimination as limiting factors within which she could define and carry out concrete and realizable objectives of social mobility.

Mrs. Sims' fatalism about what her children's futures could have been was consistent with her entire characterization of her life. She had two sons. The oldest had apparently gotten into trouble as a young adult and spent a good deal of time in prison. Although she referred to it as his having been "away," she remarked that she was just getting to know him during the last ten years that he had been at home. Her youngest son was killed in a fight when he was a teenager. Additionally, she reported having had both children out of wedlock, the first pregnancy resulting from a rape. Thus, throughout her life history, beginning with young womanhood, she presents herself as a victim. This sense of victimization pervades her story and influences her attitudes toward many aspects of her life.

Two types of childrearing goals have been identified thus far: goals regarding the child's future position in the society and goals regarding his or her personal and character development. In addition to these two types of goals, the women aspired to provide their children with some accoutrements of a middle class lifestyle. Their discussion of these desires often reflects the discrepancies between their lives and their employer's. Jewell Prieleau provides an example. She describes her employer's children as follows:

> Her children always dress nice. Whenever her daughter was going to music school or anyplace, I had to take her in a taxi. Whenever she finish, she had to be picked up. I had to go get her.

In describing her grandchildren, she said:

> I went to three nice department stores and I opened up credit
> for them so I could send them to school looking nice. I got up
> early in the morning and send them off to school. After school,
> I would pick them up in a taxi and bring them here (the job).

Mrs. Prieleau is not the only woman in this study who talked about
going into debt to give her children some of the material things that she
had never had and that were part of her image of a "better life" for her
children. Willa Murray told the following story:

> I remember when my sons wanted that record player. I said
> I'm gonna get a record player; I'm gonna do days work. But
> I had to get AC current for this record player. I called up this
> lady (her employer) and I said, "I'm goin' to Household
> Finance this morning. If they call you for a reference would
> you give me some reference?" She said, "Sure." I sat down and
> the man said come in. He said, "Miz Murray, do you have a
> co-signer?" I said no. He said, "Well, what's your collateral?"
> I said something about the furniture. He said, "Do you work?"
> I said, "Yeah. I do days work." He said, "Days work? You
> don't have a steady job?" I said, "Yes sir, days work." He said,
> "Who do you work for?" I told him. He said, "We'll see what
> we can do." He gave me the hundred and fifty dollars. I came
> home, phoned the electric company, told them they could send
> the man to put the current in.

In these statements and some of the ones quoted in this chapter, we
begin to see how the employer's style of life influenced the women's.
However, it cannot be assumed that the women's desires were merely
an outgrowth of the employer-employee relationship. The material
products which they sought were so widely available in the culture that
they should be considered general symbols of upward mobility. Upward
mobility for their children was the basic goal of most of the women
who participated in this study. It was a goal which seems to have
existed prior to and apart from their work situation and the values of
their employers. Nevertheless, in some cases the women found
reinforcement for and regeneration of these goals within the work

situation, just as they found supports within their community and family lives.

Protecting the Children

> The main thing of being a working mother is to leave your children under supervision. . . . I took [my children] to my knees and I prayed with them before I left for work and I said, I'm giving you to God and to the two neighbors and the people in the neighborhood. And they were never to leave the neighborhood without the permission of the lady on the ground floor, or the lady next door to me. The key was around their neck. I hear them talking about keys around the neck showin' a mother's working. You can work if you have proper supervision. My children knew that they had to obey everyone that was older than them regardless to who they were. . . . This is why, when I hear on the radio, it's no good for the mother to work—my mother before me had to work. My mother worked with five of us. . . . We never went to jail, and every one of us worked. But about you being a working mother . . . what do you expect from your children if you don't leave them under supervision?

During the 1940s when Willa Murray was raising her two children, social attitudes towards working mothers were considerably less supportive than they are today. Children with keys around their necks and the mothers who left home to earn wages in factories and private households were thought to be a major contributing factor to juvenile delinquency. According to Lois Hoffman and Ivan Nye, "The employment of women away from the home for any considerable period of time was believed to be incompatible with good care of the home and children."[4] Working mothers, while they might have been pitied if they were so poor that they had to go out to work, were also scorned. Black mothers could find some community support and personal consolation in the fact that a large percentage of Black women worked outside their homes and had done so, as Mrs. Murray points out, for several generations.

Nevertheless, the problem of supervising children and protecting them from the "negative influences of the street" was fundamental to all of these women's discussions of their childrearing strategies. In their life histories, the street and the city appear as images of violence, destruction, and decay, a replica of Ann Petry's theme in her 1946 novel, *The Street*, about a working mother raising her son by herself, in Harlem. Lutie, the protagonist, expressed feelings that are implicit in many of the life histories of the women in this study.

> Yes, she thought, she and Bub (her son) had to get out of 116th Street. It was a bad street. And then she thought about the other streets. It wasn't just this street that she was afraid of or that was bad. It was any street where people were packed together like sardines in a can. And it wasn't just this city. It was any city where they set up a line and say Black folks stay on this side and White folks on this side, so that the Black folks were crammed on top of each other—jammed and packed and forced into the smallest possible space until they were completely cut off from light and air.
>
> It was any place where the women had to work to support the families because the men couldn't get jobs and the men got bored and pulled out and the kids were left without proper homes because there was nobody around to put a heart into it. Yes. It was anyplace where the people were so damn poor they didn't have time to do anything but work, and their bodies were the only source of relief from the pressure under which they lived; and where the crowding together made the young girls wise beyond their years.[5]

For Lutie, as for many of the women in this study, the struggle against "the street" was a struggle against the ravages of poverty and discrimination. It was an effort to keep their goals and aspirations clearly in focus, despite the external forces that threatened them. Yet, while many participants in the study spoke abstractly about the streets of New York as a place of destruction, some described their specific neighborhood as a place of sharing and mutual concern; a community with various institutions and people who aided them in supervising their children.

Strategies for keeping the children out of trouble and for protecting them from the street varied, as is indicated in the case studies and in Mrs. Murray's comments. Community institutions and organizations, neighbors and friends, kinfolk, supportive employers, and God were all talked about as elements in this process. Another strategy was to monitor the children's friends, as much as possible. Johnnie Mae Boatwright said that she was criticized on this account.

> They said I picked his crowd. Well, I did pick the crowd. I wanted him to go with somebody that really have a good name and thought something of themselves. I didn't want him to go with a low class of girls because they had nothing to teach him. I wanted him to look up at somebody that had more than him so that he could learn something.

Mrs. Runner echoed these sentiments:

> When they go out sometimes, you overprotect them, you worry about them when they get a certain age—the environment, who they're going to come in contact with. You don't like to pick their company, because you can't. . . . You have to watch the company they keep and their associations because that means a lot. You know they can get into the wrong kind of company.

The concerns expressed about protecting the children must be looked at with particular reference to the women's aspirations for them. For most participants in this study who were seeking to help their children attain better jobs and a more comfortable life than their own, concerns about protection accompanied aspirations of upward mobility. The statements above, for example, not only reveal concerns that the children be kept out of trouble, but also that they be exposed to better things. Mrs. Boatwright, for example, is quite explicit in saying that she hoped her son would meet people who had "more than him so that he could learn something." Mrs. Prieleau's move to an integrated neighborhood in the Bronx may also be understood as an effort to both protect and uplift.

Protection becomes an important issue in the life stories of these women because they were poor and could not control or shape their environment with the same degree of freedom that their employers shaped theirs. The differential impact of income is perhaps most poignantly demonstrated in the contrast between Mrs. Prieleau's story about her own children and grandchildren and her presentation of her employer's childrearing strategies (see Chapter Three). What Mrs. Prieleau admired most was her employers' ability to provide protection for their children as a matter of course and in a manner which seemed to reinforce their other goals.

Another way employer-employee differences regarding protection are revealed is in the discussion of punishment. The women were asked whether or not they had ever punished their employer's children, the kinds of things they had punished them for, and the ways in which the children were punished. They were then asked about their own children and called upon to compare the method of punishment. Several responses were quite revealing. Mrs. Boatwright said the following about punishing her employer's children:

> MRS. BOATWRIGHT: I would make them sit in a room and they had to stay there by themselves and [I] wouldn't let them come out until a certain time. Or either, if they wanted something, I wouldn't let them have it.

> INTERVIEWER: What about your own son? Did you punish him for the same kind of misbehavior?

> MRS. BOATWRIGHT: Yes, but I punished him with a switch-end because I had to work and I couldn't tell him to stay in the house 'cause when I go away he'll go. So I had to take care of him right then, so he would know what I meant.

The distinction between reasoning with the employer's children and spanking one's own was prevalent throughout the data. Several women expressed the idea that they would not hit another person's children, while they considered it acceptable to hit their own. However, Mrs. Boatwright's statement goes beyond this simple distinction to provide us with some insight into what she saw as the particular needs of her situation; needs which arose from the fact that she was a working mother, and out of the house most of the day. Mrs. Hudson also talked about punishment and some of the differences between the lives of her employer's children and her son. She said:

> MRS. HUDSON: I spanked mine, but I didn't have to spank these (employer's) children. I could just tell them no, you can't do that, and they don't do that.

INTERVIEWER: What kinds of things would you spank them for then?

MRS. HUDSON: Oh, telling me a lie. Or going someplace and telling me a lie that you didn't go and you did go. . . . Their (employer's children) lives was a little different than mine was with my children. These children didn't go out much. They just had their little friends to go to. Now with my children, I had to know where they were going and who they were going out with.

Mrs. Hudson's struggle to protect her children from the evils of the street was dependent upon their following her instructions. It is no wonder that violations of these instructions, such as she described above, were taken so seriously. The difference then is not only that the employer's children did not go out much, but that their activities were monitored and circumscribed. Since the Hudson children were more often alone, Mrs. Hudson sought to have them internalize self-protective strategies and to have absolute respect, if not fear, of her authority, even when she was not present.

What may be derived from these examples is that the differences in social structural conditions between Mrs. Boatwright, Mrs. Hudson, and their employers required divergent sets of childrearing tactics and strategies. Melvin Kohn's model of social class and parent-child relationships provides theoretical confirmation of the contrasts we can observe in employer-employee childrearing goals and patterns.[6] Kohn argues that social class determines conditions of life which, in turn, give rise to particular sets of values suited to those conditions of life. These values then provide the framework within which parents interact with their children. Kohn's model is particularly helpful in understanding the women's own characterization of the differences between their children and their employer's children because he does not reduce these differences to a simple set of behavioral patterns characterizing each social class. Instead, his model provides a way of understanding the meaning of any particular set of behaviors within the life space of the people who perform them. In the analysis of these data we are confronted with a situation in which working class Black women participate in middle class White family life and portray themselves as exhibiting two different types of behavior towards children with different life circumstances. Astutely, they explain the differences in behavior in terms of the differences in conditions of life.

The women's presentations of the differences in childrearing techniques between themselves and their employer's is particularly revealing of these differences. Not surprisingly, the women tended to criticize their employers for not being strict enough with their own children. Pearl Runner said:

> They—the White people—seemed to use more psychology on their children and it didn't work. . . . She (the employer) was outside in the backyard talking to her friends and he spit right in her fact. See, she would use psychology; I would have—it's a good thing it wasn't me, he would have really got it. They (an employing family) use to bribe their children. They would say, now Sidney, be good and I'm gonna bring you back a toy. I'm gonna bring you this. They used to buy them, in other words, and that I didn't like. They always had to bring them back something for them to be good. . . . I believe if you're going to give the child a present, you give them, whether they're good or bad, but don't bribe them. I don't think it's a good policy because they're looking forward all the time for a gift or something and I don't think that's a good policy.

Mrs. Runner's characterization of the use of psychology in the White families for whom she worked tends to confirm Kohn's notion of the developmental and self-directive focus of middle class childrearing patterns as distinct from the emphasis upon conformity to externally imposed standards which typifies working class parenting. While Mrs. Runner is describing what she sees as lax parenting, resulting in an insolent and undisciplined child, she draws attention to the differences in expectations between herself and the child's parents. Ella Little's views follow the same pattern in discussing how surprised she was by the behavior of her various employer's children.

> I didn't allow my children to say no, I won't do this, no I won't do that. I mean I would prefer for them to come to me, talk with me, say, Mother, I don't want to do this for these reasons, and why do I have to do this. But not just stand up in your face and say no. But these White children, they would

just tell their parents no and all kinds of stuff, and the parents would give in a lot.

Throughout the data, the women identified similar types of "problems" in the employer's childrearing methods. The parents are generally described as permitting their children to be impertinent, sassy, rude, and unruly. In general, the parents were not considered strict enough because they did not impose strict standards to which the children would be required to conform. These criticisms were consistent in the women's life histories and exemplify the different life conditions and cultural experiences to which parents responded.

Raising the Children

For private household workers, who worked for middle and upper class White families, these class and racial differences in parenting occur within a relationship of inequality. The data collected in this study permit us to examine parent-child interaction as it is perceived and constructed by the household workers themselves. This has benefits as well as liabilities. As outsiders, whose childrearing practices and lifestyle differed from that of the employers, the women in this study provide a particularly revealing picture of parent-child relationships in the employing family. However, they were not mere observers of the process; they participated in it and thereby restructured it. The women's insights, therefore, offer a unique critical perspective that is only found in subordinates' characterizations of their superiors. However, as participants in the process, their observations are limited to the time frame in which they were present and make it virtually impossible to assess the women's impact on the process. Nevertheless, their stories about their own role in rearing the employer's children provide considerable understanding of how they saw their work, and, more importantly, how their work affected their own style of parenting. Willa Murray's comments below illuminate this:

Throughout, the people that I worked for taught their children that they can talk back. They would let them (the children) say anything they wanted to say to them. I noticed a lot of times they (the children) would talk back or something and they (the parents) would be hurt. They would say to me, "I wish they (the children) wouldn't. I wish they were more like your children." They allowed them to do so much. But, they taught them a lot of things. I know one thing, I think I got a lot of things from them. . . . I think I've learnt a lot about [how to do] with my children by letting them do and telling them—like the Whites would tell them—that I trust you. I think a lot of Black mothers when we come along, they didn't trust us. They were always telling us that we were gonna do. . . . But I think that they (Whites) talk to their children about what's in life, what's for them, what not to do. And they let them talk, they tell them all the things that we didn't tell our children. We're beginning to tell our children. . . . The alternative is that I told my children straight, that if a boy and a girl have sexual intercourse—I learned that from the White people—and you don't have anything to protect it, that girl will get a baby. So my children were looking out for that. I learned that from my people. I listened to what they tell [their children].

Talk, between parents and children, is a dominant theme of Mrs. Murray's comments. She is critical of the parents for permitting their children to "talk back" to them, to question their instructions, to respond impertinently or otherwise mock or demean the parents' authority. Yet, talking *with* the children, reasoning with them, explaining things and hearing their thoughts and opinions on various matters, is behavior which she admired enough to try and emulate. Telling the children that you "trust them" places greater emphasis upon self-direction than upon following orders. Clearly, the line between letting the children talk and permitting them to "talk back" is a difficult one to draw, yet Mrs. Murray draws it in transferring her work-learned behavior to her own childrearing circumstances. Her statement continues:

But most of their (Whites) children are very bold. They're rude to their parents. And so they (employers) used to like me to tell their children, because I could set 'em straight. And many of them tell me, I wish I could raise my child to be respectful as your child. Your children are so much more respectful.

It should not be surprising that there would be behavioral
characteristics which employers would admire in employee children, just
as there were traits which Mrs. Murray and others admired in their
employer's interactions with their children. In fact, it is striking that
each would admire aspects of the other and seek to incorporate them
within their own lives, while the circumstances that generated those
particular patterns were quite different. Nevertheless, reorienting the
parent-child relationship in the employer's family was frequently
described as a regular part of the worker's child care activity. In fact,
the women's discussion of their experiences in caring for their
employer's children are variations upon the stories of resistance which
characterized their establishing themselves in the employer-employee
relationship. Queenie Watkins' description of the following child care
incident provides a good example:

> One morning I was feeding Stevie oatmeal and I was eating
> oatmeal. His uncle and I were all sitting at the table together
> eating. He said, "I don't want this and I'm gonna spit it out."
> I said, "You better not, Stevie." With that he just let it all
> come into my face. I took myself a big mouthful and let it go
> right back in his face. He screamed, and his uncle said, "What
> did you do that for?" I said, "You fight fire with fire. My
> psychology is to let a child know he can't do to you what you
> can't do to him." The mother came running. I said, "This ends
> my work here," but she said, "Just wash Stevie's face." I said,
> "I'm not gonna wash it, let him wash it himself"—he wasn't
> two years old. Finally I said, "I'll take him and wash his face
> but who's gonna wash my face?" His mother started to laugh
> and said, "You're some character." And you know what, he
> never did that again. He ate his food and I never had to
> chastise Stevie about anything after that.

Zenobia King told a slightly different story about the way in which she
inserted her values into the parent-child relationship of an employing
family:

> One time the daughter went out and she stayed all day. She
> didn't tell her mother where she was. And when she came
> back, her mother jumped on her in a really bad way. She told

her she wished she had died out there, etc., etc., and her
daughter said if her mother had loved her she would have
asked where she was going. So, I separated them. I sent the
daughter to one room and the mother to the other and I talked
to both of them and I brought them back together.

In both of these stories, as in others in this genre, the women see
themselves as the instructor of both the children and the parents. They
characterize themselves as helping the parent learn how to parent while
simultaneously setting rules and regulations as to the kind of treatment
they expected from the children. Queenie Watkins' philosophy of
fighting fire with fire was reiterated by Oneida Harris, in describing her
relations with one of the children whom she cared for.

He was nine years old and he rate me the worst maid they'd
ever had because I wouldn't take any of his foolishness. If he
kicked me on the shins, I'd kick him back. . . . I said he hasn't
any bringing up, and if I stay here he's gonna listen. I said to
his mother, if you don't want me, tell me tomorrow and I'll
go. So anyway, the next day he would bring me up a little bit;
she's the next to the worst maid we ever had. Each week I
came up 'til I was the best one.

As in the stories of resistance, both Queenie Watkins and Oneida Harris
depict themselves as setting guidelines for respect from the children in
the same way respect was established in the employer-employee
relationship. The additional dimension of instructing parents in the ways
of handling their children was another recurrent theme in the life
histories. Willa Murray described a scene similar to the one which
Zenobia King related:

Now the lady I worked for called P_____, when I used to
come there to work on Saturday, the house would be in an
uproar. This child, fourteen years old, would be throwing the
furniture out of the room and telling them what she was and
wasn't gonna do. And there they stood, in awe of what to do.
All I had to do was walk in and say, "Debby, what you doing?
Put that furniture back down. This is not your house, it's your
mother's house. You only live here. You're only a child. Put
that furniture back in there." And they would tell me she's

gonna run out. I said, "Open the door and let her go, she ain't
going nowhere. This is not her house, she has no business to
treat you like this. . . ." And then they would say to me, "How
did you do it?" Now I'm the maid, not the mistress. But they
were permissive. They let their children run around.

Through these and other similar anecdotes which the women used
to describe their participation in caring for their employer's children,
they communicate a perception of their employers as uncomfortable in
exercising the power associated with their parenting role. To a large
degree, they depict their employers as either inconsistent and afraid of
their children or ignorant of childrearing strategies that would develop
obedience and respect. The women see this as their forte and in many
instances describe themselves as exercising power on behalf of the
parents, teaching the children to obey them, and to respect their parents.
In so doing they also present themselves as teaching the parents. Willa
Murray is keenly aware of the paradoxical nature of this situation when
she says, "Now I'm the maid, not the mistress." In the maid-mistress
relationship, the latter gives instructions which the former carries out.
In a sense Willa Murray's story presents a role reversal, one which she
finds both surprising and amusing but also appropriate. It is akin to an
anecdote in which she described herself telling her employers that they
had more education than she did, but their behavior was not intelligent.
These presentations suggest that despite stereotypic conceptions of the
maid-mistress relationship, women in these roles could gain
considerable power and influence within a family, particularly those
where they had worked for a number of years and had considerable
responsibility.
    The household worker's impact on the parent-child relationship is
only one aspect of their child care role. The other, equally important
aspect of this role is their relationship with the children they cared for
and the fact, implicit in their earlier discussion, that they describe
themselves as surrogate mothers for these children.

There's a long time she (the child) use to thought I was her
mama. She would ask me, "Why is my skin white and yours
brown, you my mama?" I tell her I'm not your mama, and I
see the hurt coming in her eye. You know like she didn't want

me to say that. I said there's your mama in there, I'm just your nurse. She said no, you my mama. (Mattie Washington)

I took care of the children. In fact, the children would call me when they had a problem or something, before they would call her (their mother). Zenobia King

He (the boy) looked at me as a mother. When he went away to school, he just would not come home if I wasn't there. And even when he was at home, if he was out playing with the boys, he'd come in, his mother, grandmother and father would be sitting around, he'd say, where is everybody? His mother would look around and say well if you mean Oneida, I think she's upstairs. Upstairs he'd come. And they couldn't get that. It was sad, you see. They give him everything in the world but love. (Oneida Harris)

I was more like a mother to them and you see she didn't have to take too much time as a mother should to know her children. They were more used to me because I put them to bed. The only time she would actually be with them was like when I'm off Thursdays and on Sundays. They would go out sometime, but actually I was really the mother because I raised them from little. (Pearl Runner)

Without exception, the women in this study who had child care responsibilities talked about themselves as being "like a mother" to their employer's children. Their explanations of the development of this kind of relationship tended to follow that of Oneida Harris and Pearl Runner: their employers were frequently unavailable and spent less time with the children than they did. Because they interacted with the children on a daily basis and often had responsibility for their care, discipline, play, and meals, their role was a vital and important one in the eyes of both child and parent. This explains, in part, some of their power in affecting the parent-child relationship, as discussed above. The fact that the women had such an important and pivotal role in the development of the employer's children and at the same time held a job in which they could be replaced gave the entire relationship of parent, child, and housekeeper a particularly intense quality. For the most part, workers developed their strongest emotional ties to the children in the employing family. Johnetta Freeman's story about her pain in leaving the children in an otherwise unpleasant job gives us a sense of the conflicting emotions that child care in housework could generate.

> I left [the job when] it got on my nerves, I couldn't take it no more. She (the employer) tried to compromise and she just begged me [to stay]. The mister, he was there that morning and he didn't think I was gonna go. So I got my things together and I kissed the kids and said goodbye. The kids put their arms around me and just cried. I felt so bad for them but I had done made my mind up. I said, "Now I'm gonna go," and they kept holding my coattail, just pulling me back and hollering. I felt so bad.

Because the women saw themselves as surrogate mothers, the children for whom they cared could easily become their surrogate children. This is particularly apparent when we compare their comments and discussion about their own and their employer's children. One of the most prevalent patterns was to talk with pride and satisfaction about the accomplishments of their surrogate children. In general, the women would talk about how frequently they heard from these children and whether they got cards, letters, or money at Mother's Day or Christmas. In addition, they'd describe the (now grown) children's occupation and family and, if they had pictures available, they would show them to me. This type of commentary provided an interesting parallel to their discussions of their own children. But even more important, it was designed to communicate the closeness that they felt existed between them and the children they had raised; closeness which was maintained over a number of years even after the children were grown.

Surrogate mothering, as pointed out in Opallou Tucker's case study, had the prospect of tying the worker into the emotional life of the employing family. For women who lived outside the employer's household and were actively engaged in rearing and caring for their own children, as were most of the women in this study, the prospect was minimized. However, for a woman like Mattie Washington, who lived-in for most of the thirty years that she worked for one family, the potential for being enveloped in their life at the expense of her own was much greater.

Living-in was not the sole cause of Mrs. Washington's intense involvement in her employer's family. She endured a long-term separation from her own child and never lived with members of her family of procreation during these years. (Unlike Mrs. Prieleau who, though separated from her daughter, remarried briefly and also had her child and grandchildren with her after some time.) All of these things combined to make Mrs. Washington's reliance on the Salzoff family, and her relationship with their daughter Ellen, assume great personal significance.

Mrs. Washington talked a lot about Ellen in her life-history. She described Ellen's job and the kinds of secrets they used to share and keep from Ellen's mother when she was growing up. But a more profound comment on this relationship was found in Mrs. Washington's reply to a question about why she never remarried after separating from her husband in 1940. She said:

I don't know, crazy I guess, 'cause I met a nice fellow since I've been here, could have been married and living on easy street. I was still working for the same people I'm working for now. I was sleeping in. I think I thought more of Ellen, figured they'd mistreat her. I knowed they wouldn't but I just didn't want to leave Ellen. I didn't want to take no time off to be with this fellow.

Mrs. Washington's reluctance to leave her employer's child, in light of the fact that she had left her own child, is a significant indication of the intimacies and dependencies that could develop between employer and employee, particularly where children were concerned. At some level, Ellen became a substitute for her own daughter, and Mattie Washington found that she could do in that relationship some of the things that distance and money prevented her from doing with her own child. Throughout her life history, Mrs. Washington communicates her feeling that her employers cared more about her and were nicer to her than many other people had been in her life. She had left the South when her daughter was just a toddler and after her husband had deserted her. She came North in search of better opportunities and a change in environment. After searching, she found security and a mothering relationship in the Salzoff family. In many ways, those things were enough to encourage her to—as she put it—"give them most my youth life."

Mattie Washington's story is a classic in domestic work, but it is not typical or in any way representative of the stories told by other women who participated in this study. It is, instead, an extreme example of the kinds of ties employees could develop with their employer's family and must be explained, in part, by Mrs. Washington's personal needs as well as her work situation. Her story also indicated how much the development of a surrogate mother-child relationship depended upon and affected all other aspects of the worker's life.

With the exception of two women, those who participated in this study did not live-in but lived in their own households and did days work. Thus, while they present themselves as surrogate mothers, their descriptions of their relationship with the employer's children bears only very general similarity to Mrs. Washington's case. In most instances, the women described themselves as caretakers, playmates, disciplinarians, confidantes, and friends of the employer's children. Nevertheless, it is clear from their discussion that in most cases the real ties of affection between themselves and their employer came through the children.

The children, therefore, provided both the ties that bound the women to their employers as well as the mark of their difference. The role of surrogate mother allowed the women to cross over these barriers, and for a fleeting moment express their love and concern for a child without regard to the obstacles that lay ahead. Also, because most young children readily return love that is freely given and are open and accepting of people without regard to status factors that have meaning for their parents, the workers probably felt that they were treated with greater equality and more genuine acceptance by the children of the household. Finally, the women could potentially develop a "special" role in relationship to their charges: that of interpreting and explaining racial conflict and differences. Chaplin has suggested that this was a byproduct of the Black household worker's relationship with her White employer's children.[7] While this issue was not explored at length in this study, there are some indications that this kind of interaction took place among those workers who had long-term relationships with an employer's children. Lena Hudson provided an example of how she helped one of her employer's sons come to terms with racial prejudice.

He (the employer's son) said to me, "Lena, I think my grandmother is prejudiced." She didn't want him to bring his little colored friend over to dinner. He said, "I'm gonna break her though. I'm gonna break her." I said to him, "Now listen, you might lose your grandmother's friendship. You'll never break her. What she know about Black people is what she read. And they don't always get the best books on the Blacks. Far as your grandmother's feelings, she don't think a Black person have any brains."

So they did come to me with things like that, see. And I say, you'll never break her, but you can lose her friendship, so you better let it stay just like it is. I thought that was the best way to leave it because he felt very bad about it.

NOTES

1. Drake and Cayton, p. 246.
2. Ibid.
3. W. E. B. DuBois, *Darkwater* (New York: Harcourt, Brace & Howe, 1920), p. 110.
4. Lois Hoffman and Ivan Nye, *Working Mothers* (San Francisco: Jossey-Bass, 1974), p. 11.
5. Ann Petry, *The Street* (New York: Pyramid Books, 1946), p. 130.
6. Melvin Kohn, "Social Class and Parent-Child Relationships," *American Journal of Sociology*, 73 (January, 1963), pp. 471-480.
7. Chaplin, *Rationalization*, pp. 7-9.

CHAPTER SIX

CONCLUSIONS

Too often discussions of domination and oppression leave the reader with the belief that the oppressed are either helpless and defeated victims of selfish and greedy oppressors, or brave and self-sacrificing revolutionaries risking their lives for the cause of freedom. The women who participated in this study were neither of these, though we might surmise that at times they could sympathize or identify with both. Instead, their stories chronicle a balancing act, a walk on a tightrope with the loss of an independent personal life on one side and the loss of the means of subsistence on the other. For the most part, they acknowledged these constraints without acquiescing to them; they simultaneously accepted and resisted their social role.

On the one hand, they were freedom fighters. Women who fought without guns or picket signs, but used the weapons they had honed for years in the households of their employers: patience, negotiation, craftiness, observation, imitation, and criticism. They fought for respect from their employers and sought to achieve for their children and grandchildren what they could not achieve for themselves: a complete release from the stigma of domestic service. Their childrearing goals and strategies, therefore, were an extension of their perceptions of themselves and their work. Through the subsequent generations, most of their fondest hopes and aspirations were affirmed. The ability to free their children from their lifelong struggle was their measure of success and achievement.

On the other hand, they were conciliators, teaching their Black children that all White people were not bad and their White employers' children that some Black people could love and care for them almost as if they were their own. Some used the opportunity to sensitize their employers' children to the plight of Black people. But apparently this was done quietly and as a response to the children's inquiries rather than by their own insistence. Through years of working with one family, helping the children learn and grow, seeing the mistress' weaknesses as

well as her strengths, resentment and anger about the disparities
between the two families became lost in a kind of bizarre kinship of
shared experiences. The intimacy of the employer-employee relationship
diluted the strength of the women's protests, and the women settled into
their jobs as they would settle into a marriage. They learned to accept
and adjust to the little indignities they could not change. Changing jobs
was a pattern early in one's career in household service. If you did not
leave the occupation, you found the "best" situation possible and made
it as good as you could make it. You became a negotiator.

The intimacy of the employer-employee relationship diffused some
of the fire and anger of youth, and was a great threat to the worker's
autonomy and independence. For, as Katzman pointed out:

> Employers could also use the intimacy of the mistress/servant
> relationship to exploit the affection and sympathy which a
> servant developed for her mistress.[1]

Thus, women quickly learned to resist the employer's attempts to
subsume them into the daily operation of the household. Having
families of their own with whom they lived was an important anchor,
especially if their family offered the economic support of an additional
income. Among the participants in this study, married women who lived
with their husbands appeared to have had the greater freedom in
choosing employers and interacting with them than those who were the
sole support of their household. Nevertheless, family life, for all of the
women, provided a kind of emotional and cultural life-jacket that kept
the worker from being washed away in a sea of employer needs and
demands. This, in combination with church and some civic activities
provided an alternative social reference for the worker. Her community
provided an alternative perspective on the dignity of her work; and her
church, the one community institution to which almost all of the
participants in this study belonged, provided opportunities for status and
recognition that were largely unrelated to her work.

If these women's lives are any indication, the preference of Black
women towards live-out work takes on even greater meaning. Katzman
attributed the shift from live-in to live-out housework to the increasing
participation of Black women in the occupation outside the South. He
argued that this was one way the workers themselves changed the
occupation.[2] The women who participated in this study showed a

definite preference for live-out work. Some had lived-in when they were younger, and like most domestic servants, complained about the confinement and isolation they encountered. The two mothers in this study who worked as live-in housekeepers with a single family over a long period of time endured separations from their children primarily because they had no childcare arrangements in the North and thought that live-in work would enable them to save money and provide greater financial support and their children. The parallels between the lives of these women, Jewell Prieleau and Mattie Washington, are striking. Both of them, at times, submerged their own needs for an independent personal life to the needs of their employers. Mattie Washington would not remarry and leave her employer's child to be cared for by someone else although she had earlier left her own child. Jewell Prieleau remarried, but continued to live-in with her employer and the marriage did not last. Their daughters, separated from their mothers for their entire childhood, both suffered some kind of emotional instability as adults. Mattie Washington's daughter had a nervous breakdown. Jewell Prieleau's daughter became an alcoholic. These patterns do not permit us to confirm causality, but they do confirm an important relationship between work and family. Without the immediacy of family, particularly dependent children, a woman was more likely to let her employer's family meet her wishes to nurture, and be part of daily family life. The employer thereby won "a faithful and loyal servant, one who lost her own vision of an independent life and instead adopted the family she worked for as a substitute for her own."[3]

Nevertheless, an analysis of these lives over time suggests that this was not a permanent condition. Later in life when the employer's children were grown, the two women who had lived-in, both Mrs. Washington and Mrs. Prieleau, rented their own living quarters, outside the employer's household. Even if they did not stay there every night, they saw their residence as a place to go, to get away from their employers, to entertain their friends, and to be an independent person. Jewell Prieleau and Mattie Washington looked back over their lives with regret and acknowledged the personal pitfalls of their ties to their employer's family. The fact that they did finally move out suggests that their submersion in the other family was never complete, that the recognition of their role and the differences between them and their employers was a constant, underlying tension, always reminding them that they were only "*like* one of the family."[4]

One of the issues which this study has sought to answer is the relationship of race and class in these women's lives. What makes their experiences different from the experiences of any other household worker? Where do racial factors begin and class factors end in defining their experiences? What did it mean to be a domestic servant and particularly what did it mean to be a Black domestic servant?

I have tried to suggest throughout the analysis of the data that many of the women's feelings and experiences were reflective of the nature of the work itself, of its position in the social structure, of its identification as women's work, and of its stigma as menial, degrading labor. Yet, part of the reason why it was so stigmatized was that it was identified with immigrants and Blacks who could do nothing else because they had few other opportunities. I have, therefore, sought to present the subtle ways racial differences operated to maintain the worker's inferior position and to act as constant reminders of the differences between the two families. Race and class were tightly bound, interacting facets in the lives of the women who participated in this study, and a careful reading of the data demonstrates their sensitivities to both as restrictive of their life chances.

Nevertheless, Black female private household workers differed from their non-Black immigrant and native-born sisters of the same generation in a number of ways. First, White private household workers received job preference over Blacks. They were generally paid more and had access to the better jobs. Black women in general and the women who participated in this study were aware that even in a low-status occupation their opportunities were limited. Second, for most White women, the occupation was a stepping stone to industrial jobs, clerical jobs, or to marriage. The women who participated in this study, as most other Black domestic servants of their generation, found themselves locked behind a racial caste barrier which offered no immediate escape. They could not use the occupation as a personal stepping stone and therefore made themselves the stepping stone for their children. Third, marriage did not guarantee a Black woman that she would not have to work. In fact, because Black men faced economic discrimination in the marketplace, married Black women often had to work in order to make ends meet. Thus, to a much larger extent than their White counterparts, Black female domestic servants tended to work while married and raising their children.

The women who participated in this study were selected in order to reveal more about the ways women managed these two families. What their life stories have demonstrated is that family life was both an independent and a dependent variable in relationship to work. First, it shaped the nature of the women's participation in the work, the type of job they chose, their degree of involvement with the job and the employers. Second, it was influenced by the work, by the needs and demands of the employers, the attractions of wealth and prosperity, and the concrete assistance that employers could provide for a worker's family.

The relationship between employer and employee in domestic service is first and foremost a class relationship. It has been that way throughout these women's lives and there is no clear indication that it will change. By the same token, racial factors were always operative, for the women as a group as well as for the individual women in this study. The legacy of slavery and the lack of opportunity associated with domestic service for Black women made its stigma one that was keenly felt and required valiant and sustained resistance.

NOTES

1. Katzman, p. 176.
2. Ibid., p. 272.
3. Ibid., p. 269.
4. This phrase is the title of a fictional work about domestics by Alice Childress, *Like One of the Family* (Brooklyn, New York: Independence Publishers, 1956).

BIBLIOGRAPHY

Allen, Annie Winsor. "Both Sides of the Servant Question." *Social Services Series Bulletin* 29, American Unitarian Association, Cal., 1913.

Anderson, C. Arnold, and Bowman, Mary Jean. "The Vanishing Servant and the Contemporary Status System of the American South." *American Journal of Sociology* 59 (November 1953):215-223.

Aries, Phillipe. *Centuries of Childhood.* New York: Vintage Books, 1962.

Baker, Ella, and Cooke, Marvel. "The Bronx Slave Market." *The Crisis: A Record of the Darker Races* 42 (November 1935):330-331, 340.

Becker, Howard S. *Sociological Work.* Chicago: Aldine, 1970.

Berch, Bettina. "The Sphinx in the Household: A New Look at the History of Household Workers." *Review of Radical Political Economics* 16 (Spring 1984):1:pp. 105-120.

Blackwell, James. *The Black Community.* New York: Dodd, Mead, & Co., 1975.

Bogle, Donald. *Toms, Coons, Mulattoes, Mammies, and Bucks.* New York: Viking Press, 1973.

Brewer, Mason J. *American Negro Folklore.* Chicago: Quadrangle Books, 1968.

Brown, Elsa Barkley. "The Legacy of Black Domestic Workers: Laboring and Organizing." Presented at the Oxford College of Humanities Lecture Series, Oxford, Georgia. Available:

145

Binghamton, NY: State University of New York at Binghamton, 1986.

Brown, Jean Collier. *Concerns of Household Workers*. New York: The Women's Press, 1941.

Brown, Jean Collier. *Household Workers*. Chicago: Science Research Associates, 1940.

Center for Research on Women. "Selected Social Science Readings on Household Workers/Domestic Workers." Booklet. Memphis, Tenn.: Memphis State University, 1992.

Chaney, Elsa M. and Castro, Mary Garcia. *Muchachas No More: Household Workers in Latin America and the Caribbean.* Philadelphia: Temple University Press, 1989.

Chaplin, David. "Domestic Service and the Negro." In *Blue Collar World.* Edited by Arthur Shostak and William Gamberg. Englewood Cliffs, N.J.: Prentice-Hall, 1964.

Chaplin, David. "Domestic Service and the Rationalization of Household Economy." Paper presented at the American Sociological Association Annual Meetings, 1969.

Chaplin, David. "The Employment of Domestic Servants as a Class Indicator: A Methodological Discussion." Paper presented at the Social Science History Association Meeting, Philadelphia, Penn., October 1976.

Childress, Alice. *Like One of the Family*. Brooklyn, New York: Independence Publishers, 1956.

Cicourel, Aaron V. *Method and Measurement in Sociology*. New York: Free Press of Glencoe, 1964.

Clark-Lewis, Elizabeth. "This Work Had A 'End': The Transition From Live-in to Day Work." Available: Memphis, Tenn.: Memphis State University Center for Research on Women, 1985.

Clark-Lewis, Elizabeth. "From Servant to Household Worker." In *To Toil the Livelong Day: America's Women at Work.* Edited by Mary Beth Norton and Carol Groneman. Ithaca, N.Y.: Cornell University Press, 1987.

Cock, Jacklyn. *Maids and Madams: A Study in the Politics of Exploitation.* Johannesburg: Raven Press, 1980.

Colen, Shellee. "With Respect and Feeling: Voices of West Indian Child Care and Domestic Workers in New York City." In *All American Women: Lines that Divide, Ties that Bind.* Edited by Johnetta B. Cole. New York: The Free Press, 1986.

Coles, Jane Hallowell, and Coles, Robert. *Women of Crisis.* New York: Delacorte Press, 1978.

Davidoff, Lenore. "Mastered for Life: Servant, Wife and Mother in Victorian and Edwardian England." *Journal of Social History* 7 (Summer 1974):406-428.

Denzin, Norman K. *The Research Act.* Chicago: Aldine, 1970.

Dill, Bonnie Thornton. "The Means to Put My Children Through: Child Rearing Goals and Stratgies Among Black Female Domestic Servants. In *The Black Woman.* Edited by La Francis Rodgers-Rose. Beverly Hills, Cal.: Sage Press, 1980.

Dill, Bonnie Thornton. "Making Your Job Good Yourself: Domestic Service and the Construction of Personal Identity." In *Women and the Politics of Empowerment.* Edited by Ann Bookman and Sandra Morgen. Philadelphia: Temple University Press, 1988.

Dill, Bonnie Thornton, and Joslin, Daphne. "The Limits of Quantitative Methods: The Need for Life Histories." Paper presented at the

Society for the Study of Social Problems Annual Meetings, Chicago, September 1977.

Drake, St. Clair, and Cayton, Horace. *Black Metropolis*. New York: Harper and Row, 1945.

DuBois, W. E. B. *Darkwater*. New York: Harcourt, Brace & Howe, 1920.

DuBois, W. E. B. *The Philadelphia Negro*. 1899; reprint ed., New York: Schocken Books, 1967.

Dudden, Faye E. *Serving Women: Household Service in Nineteenth Century America*. Middletown, Conn.: Wesleyan University Press, 1983.

Eaton, Isabel. "Negro Domestic Service in Seventh Ward Philadelphia." In *The Philadelphia Negro*. By W. E. B. DuBois. New York: Schocken Books, 1967.

Ellis, Benson. *A Socio-economic Study of the Female Domestic Worker in Private Homes With Special Reference to New York City*. New York: Department of Investigation, 1939.

Genovese, Eugene. *Roll, Jordan, Roll*. New York: Pantheon, 1974.

Glaser, Barney, and Strauss, Anselm. *The Discovery of Grounded Theory*. Chicago: Aldine, 1967.

Goffman, Erving. *Stigma*. Englewood Cliffs, N.J.: Prentice-Hall, 1963.

Glenn, Evelyn Nakano. *Nisei, Issei, Warbride: Three Generations of Japanese American Women in Domestic Service*. Philadelphia: Temple University Press, 1986.

Glenn, Evelyn Nakano. "Women, Labor Migration and Household Work: Japanese American Women in the Pre-War Period." In *Ingredients for Women's Employment Policy*. Edited by Christine Bose and Glenna Spitze. Albany, N.Y.: SUNY Books, 1987.

Green, Lorenzo J., and Woodson, Carter G. *The Negro Wage Earner*. Washington, D.C.: The Association for the Study of Negro Life and History, Inc., 1930.

Hareven, Tamara. "Modernization and Family History: Perspectives on Social Change." *Signs* 2 (August 1976):190-206.

Haynes, Elizabeth Ross. "Negroes in Domestic Service in the United States." *Journal of Negro History* 8 (October 1923):384-442.

Haynes, George. *The Negro at Work in New York City: A Study in Economic Progress*. New York: Longman's, Green, and Co., 1912.

Hoffman, Lois, and Nye, Ivan. *Working Mothers*. San Francisco: Jossey-Bass, 1974.

Hughes, C. Everett. "The Study of Occupations." In *Sociology Today: Problems and Prospects*. Edited by Robert K. Merton, L. Broom, and L. S. Cottrell, Jr. New York: Harper Torchbooks, 1965.

Hunter, Tera. "The Politics of Household Labor in the New South." Presented: Organization of American Historians Annual Meeting, Louisville, Kentucky, 1991.

Joslin, Daphne. "Working Class Daughters, Middle Class Wives: Social Identity and Self-Esteem Among Women Upwardly Mobile Through Marriage." Ph.D. dissertation, New York University, 1979.

Katzman, David J. *Seven Days a Week*. New York: Oxford University Press, 1978.

Kohn, Melvin. "Social Class and Parent-Child Relationships." *American Journal of Sociology* 73 (January 1963):471-480.

Kousha, Mahnaz. "Race, Class and Intimacy Relationships Between Black Private Household Workers and White Mistresses." Available: Memphis, Tenn.: Memphis State University Center for Research on Women, 1992.

Lasch, Christopher. *Haven in a Heartless World.* New York: Basic Books, 1977.

Laslett, Barbara. "The Family as Public and Private Institution: An Historical Perspective." *Journal of Marriage and the Family* 35 (August 1973):480-494.

Leashore, Bogart R. "Black Female Workers: Live-in Domestics in Detroit, Michigan, 1860-1880." *Phylon* 45 (June 1984):2:111-120.

Lerner, Gerda, ed. *Black Women in White America.* New York: Pantheon Books, 1972.

McBride, Theresa. *The Romantic Revolution.* New York: Homes and Meier, 1976.

Magnus, Erna. "The Social, Economic and Legal Conditions of Domestic Servants: I & II." *International Labor Review* 30 (August 1934):109-207 and 30 (September 1934):336-364.

Malveaux, Julianne M. "From Domestic Worker to Household Technician: Black Women in a Changing Occupation." In *Black Women in the Labor Force.* Edited by Phyllis A. Wallace. Cambridge, Mass.: MIT Press, 1980.

Memmi, Albert. *Dominated Man.* Boston: Beacon Press, 1968.

Memmi, Albert. *The Colonizer and the Colonized.* Boston, Beacon Press, 1965.

Merton, Robert, and Kendall, Patricia L. "The Focused Interview." *American Journal of Sociology* 51 (May 1946):541-557.

Noble, Jeanne L. *An Exploratory Study of Domestics' View of Their Working World.* Report prepared for the Office of Manpower Policy, Evaluation and Research, U. S. Department of Labor, Manpower Administration, 1967. (Mimeographed.)

Oakley, Ann. *The Sociology of Housework.* New York, Pantheon Books, 1974.

Olney, James. *Metaphors of Self.* Princeton, N.J.: Princeton University Press, 1972.

Ovington, Mary White. *Half a Man.* New York: Longman's, Green, and Co., 1911; reprint ed., New York: Schocken Books, 1969.

Palmer, Phyllis M. "Housework and Domestic Labor: Racial and Technological Change." In *My Troubles are Going to Have Trouble with Me.* Edited by Karen Sacks and Dorothy Remy. New Brunswick, NJ: Rutgers University Press, 1984.

Palmer, Phyllis M. *Domesticity and Dirt: Housewives and Domestic Servants in the United States, 1920-1945.* Philadelphia: Temple University Press, 1990.

Parsons, Talcott, and Bales, Robert. *The Family: Socialization and Interaction Process.* Glencoe, Ill.: Free Press, 1955.

Pessar, Patricia R. "The Linkage Between the Household and Workplace in the Experience of Dominican Immigrant Women in the U.S." *International Migration Review* 18 (Winter 1984):4:1188-1212.

Petry, Ann. *The Street.* New York: Pyramid Books, 1946.

Rollins, Judith. "The Social Psychology of the Relationship Between Black Female Domestic Servants and their White Female Employers." Ph.D. dissertation, Brandeis University, 1983.

Rollins, Judith. *Between Women: Domestics and Their Employers.* Philadelphia: Temple University Press, 1985.

Romero, Mary. "Sisterhood and Domestic Service: Race, Class and Gender in the Mistress-Maid Relationship." *Humanity and Society* 12 (1988)4:318-346.

Romero, Mary. "Not Just Like One of the Family: Chicana Domestics Establishing Professional Relationships with Employers." *Feminist Issues* (Fall 1990) 10:2:33-42.

Romero, Mary. *Maid in the U.S.A.* New York: Routledge Press.

Rubin, Lillian. *Worlds of Pain.* New York: Basic Books, 1976.

Rubinow, I. M. "The Problem of Domestic Service." *The Journal of Political Economy* 14 (October 1906):502-519.

Ruiz, Vicki L. "By the Day or Week: Mexicana Domestic Workers in El Paso." In *Women on the United States-Mexican Border.* Edited by Vicki L. Ruiz and Susan Beth Tiano. Winchester, Mass.: Allen and Unwin.

Salmon, Lucy M. *Domestic Service.* New York: The Macmillan Co., 1897.

Selltiz, Claire; Jahoda, Marie; Deutsch, Morton; and Cook, Stuart. *Research Methods in Social Relations.* New York: Holt, Rinehart and Winston, 1959.

Sennett, Richard. *Families Against the City.* New York: Vintage Books, 1970.

Sennett, Richard, and Cobb, Jonathan. *The Hidden Injuries of Class.* New York: Knopf, 1972.

Shaw, Clifford. *The Jack Roller.* Chicago: University of Chicago Press, 1966.

Smith, Margo. "Domestic Service as a Channel of Upward Mobility for the Lower-Class Woman: The Lima Case." In *Female and Male in Latin America.* Edited by Ann Pescatello. Pittsburgh: University of Pittsburgh Press, 1973.

Stigler, George J. *Domestic Servants in the United States: 1900-1940*. Occasional Paper No. 24. New York: National Bureau of Economic Research, 1946.

Strasser, Susan M. "Mistress and Maid, Employer and Employee: Domestic Service Reform in the United States, 1897-1920." *Marxist Perspectives* (1978) 1:4:52-67.

Sutherland, Daniel. *Americans and Their Servants: Domestic Service in the United States from 1800 to 1920*. Baton Rouge, La.: Louisana State University Press, 1981.

Sutherland, Edwin H. *The Professional Thief*. Chicago: University of Chicago Press, 1937.

Thomas, W. I., and Znaniecki, Florian. *The Polish Peasant in Europe and America*. Boston: The Gorham Press, 1918.

Trieman, Donald J., and Terrell, Kermit. "Women, Work and Wages— Trends in the Female Occupation Structure." In *Social and Indicator Models*. Edited by Kenneth C. Land and Seymour Spilerman. New York: Russell Sage Foundation, 1975.

Tucker, Susan. "A Complex Bond: Southern Black Domestic Workers and Their White Employers." *Frontiers* (1987) 9:3:6-13.

Tucker, Susan. *Telling Memories Among Southern Women: Domestic Workers and Their Employers in the Segregated South*. Baton Rouge, La.: Lousiana State University Press, 1988.

U. S. Department of Labor, Employment Standards Administration. *Private Household Workers*, 1974.

U. S. Department of Labor, U. S. Employment Service. *Job Descriptions for Domestic Service and Personal Service Occupations*. Washington, D.C.: U. S. Government Printing Office, 1941.

U. S. Department of Labor, Women's Bureau, *Negro Woman Worker*, by Jean Collier Brown. Bulletin No. 165. Washington, D.C.: Government Printing Office, 1938.

INDEX

Anderson, C. Arnold, 13, 14

Baker, Ella, 104
Becker, Howard S., 23
Black community, 79
    attitudes towards domestic
        work, 85
Bowman, Mary J., 13, 14

Cayton, Horace, 40n, 112, 113
Chaplin, David, 17
Child care, 11, 119, 130, 132,
    133
Children
    character development of,
        45, 117
    discipline of employer's,
        125–129
    discipline of own, 125–129
    educational goals for, 45,
        114–116
    latchkey, 70
    protection of, 44–45, 63–64,
        122–126
Childrearing, 119–120
    goals and strategies, 4, 45
    discipline in, 53, 125–129
Childress, Alice, 143n
Church
    role in childrearing, 45, 64
Cicourel, Aaron V., 33
Coles, Jane Hallowell, 61
Coles, Robert, 61
Cook, Stuart, 32
Cooke, Marvel, 104

Data analysis
    approaches, 38
    "problematics," generation
        of, 39
Davidoff, Lenore, 20n
Days work, 6, 12, 69, 121
Denzin, Norman K., 23
Deutsch, Morton, 32
Domestic service
    ambivalence about, 83
    careers in, 39, 89, 97,
        100–102
    defined, 18n
    and fertility, 28
    and housework, 5
    importance of
        interpersonal skills in, 88
    job tenure in, 30
    non-career workers in,
        98–99
    and protective labor
        legislation, 8
    and race in the Southern
        U.S., 12–13
    and self-respect, 10, 33
    slave markets in, 101
    slavery, legacy of, 12, 100
    social status of, 4, 8
    and stigma, 30, 80, 142
    unionization and collective
        bargaining, 7–8, 18n
    and upward mobility, 114
    women's place in the family
        and, 5